Favorite American Poems

Edited by
Paul Negri

DOVER PUBLICATIONS, INC.
Mineola, New York

Bibliographical Note

Favorite American Poems is a new work, first pub-
lished by Dover Publications, Inc., in 2002.

Library of Congress Cataloging-in-Publication Data

Favorite American Poems / edited by Paul Negri.
     p. cm. — (Dover large print editions)
   ISBN-13: 978-0-486-42252-7
   ISBN-10: 0-486-42252-6
   1. American poetry. 2. Large type books. I. Negri, Paul.
II. Series.

PS586 .F38 2002
811.008—dc21

                                        2002067552

Manufactured in the United States by Courier Corporation
42252606   2014
www.doverpublications.com

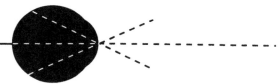

**This Large Print Book carries the
Seal of Approval of N.A.V.H.**

Note

Why poetry? Why bother with what poet Marianne Moore called "all this fiddle"? Poetry can be difficult, obscure, frustrating, even maddening. Often we have to struggle to understand, to relate the poet's ideas to our own, to find meaning in another's sometimes seemingly arbitrary arrangements of words and sounds, rhythms and rhymes.

The answer is that we read poetry because, at its best, it lives and sings. The finest verse encapsulates moments of experience in original ways that open the doors of perception. Poetry is the distilled wisdom of the race, set down in words that inform and inspire, that exalt the beauty of everyday things, that let us see life in a different light, that probe the deepest nooks and crannies of the human heart. Adrienne Rich observed that "poetry can break open locked chambers of possibility, restore numbed zones to feeling, [and] recharge desire."

The reasons we read poetry are wonderfully embodied in the perennially popular poems in

iii

this collection. Spanning more than 350 years, they comprise a treasury of verse by American poets that has stood the test of time—from Colonial poet Anne Bradstreet's heartfelt paean to her husband, to the modernist ironies of T. S. Eliot and Wallace Stevens. In between lies a rich and varied landscape of odes, dialect verse, lyrics, sonnets, and more by Walt Whitman, Emily Dickinson, Robert Frost, Carl Sandburg, Vachel Lindsay, William Carlos Williams, Ezra Pound, Edna St. Vincent Millay, Paul Laurence Dunbar, Gertrude Stein, and many others.

Almost all the stalwarts of American poetry are here, along with such lesser-known poets as Jones Very and Frances E. W. Harper, whose works live on though their names have faded. So dip into this collection and discover the ever-green wellsprings of poetry's appeal. As Andrew Carroll put it, ". . . poetry is about truth. And passion. And wisdom and love and wonder and creativity. In short—everything that makes life worthwhile."

Contents

John Greenleaf Whittier

Edgar Allan Poe

Oliver Wendell Holmes, Sr.

Jones Very

Henry David Thoreau

Herman Melville

Julia Ward Howe

Walt Whitman

Anne Bradstreet (1612?–1672)

An early colonist in Massachusetts, Bradstreet was also America's first published poet, the wife and daughter of governors of the Massachusetts Bay Colony, and a mother of eight.

To My Dear and Loving Husband

If ever two were one, then surely we.
If ever man were loved by wife, then thee.
If ever wife was happy in a man,
Compare with me, ye women, if you can.
I prize thy love more than whole mines of gold,
Or all the riches that the East doth hold.
My love is such that rivers cannot quench,
Nor ought but love from thee give recompense.
Thy love is such I can no way repay;
The heavens reward thee manifold I pray.
Then while we live, in love let's so persevere
That when we live no more, we may live ever.

Phillis Wheatley (1753?–1784)

Wheatley was a literary phenomenon: a young female slave (later freed) who wrote poetry—styled after Milton and Pope—in an adopted tongue. Her poems brought her fame both in America and abroad.

From To the Right Honourable William, Earl of Dartmouth

Should you, my lord, while you peruse my song,
Wonder from whence my love of *Freedom* sprung,
Whence flow these wishes for the common good,
By feeling hearts alone best understood,
I, young in life, by seeming cruel fate
Was snatch'd from *Afric's* fancy'd happy seat:
What pangs excruciating must molest,
What sorrows labour in my parent's breast?
Steel'd was that soul and by no misery mov'd
That from a father seiz'd his babe belov'd:
Such, such my case. And can I then but pray
Others may never feel tyrannic sway?

William Cullen Bryant (1794–1878)

An editor, translator, and abolitionist, Bryant was so revered in his time that flags in New York were lowered to half-mast at his death. "Thanatopsis" ("Meditation on Death") was first published when the poet was seventeen.

Thanatopsis

To him who in the love of Nature holds
Communion with her visible forms, she speaks
A various language; for his gayer hours
She has a voice of gladness, and a smile
And eloquence of beauty, and she glides
Into his darker musings, with a mild
And gentle sympathy, that steals away
Their sharpness, ere he is aware. When thoughts
Of the last bitter hour come like a blight
Over thy spirit, and sad images
Of the stern agony, and shroud, and pall,
And breathless darkness, and the narrow house,
Make thee to shudder, and grow sick at heart;—
Go forth, under the open sky, and list
To Nature's teachings, while from all around—
Earth and her waters, and the depths of air,—
Comes a still voice—Yet a few days, and thee
The all-beholding sun shall see no more
In all his course; nor yet in the cold ground,
Where thy pale form was laid, with many tears,
Nor in the embrace of ocean shall exist
Thy image. Earth, that nourished thee, shall claim
Thy growth, to be resolved to earth again;
And, lost each human trace, surrendering up
Thine individual being, shalt thou go
To mix forever with the elements,
To be a brother to the insensible rock
And to the sluggish clod, which the rude swain

Turns with his share, and treads upon. The oak
Shall send his roots abroad, and pierce thy mould.
Yet not to thy eternal resting place
Shalt thou retire alone—nor couldst thou wish
Couch more magnificent. Thou shalt lie down
With patriarchs of the infant world—with kings,
The powerful of the earth—the wise, the good,
Fair forms, and hoary seers of ages past,
All in one mighty sepulchre.—The hills
Rock-ribbed and ancient as the sun,—the vales
Stretching in pensive quietness between;
The venerable woods—rivers that move
In majesty, and the complaining brooks
That make the meadows green; and poured
    round all,
Old ocean's gray and melancholy waste,—
Are but the solemn decorations all
Of the great tomb of man. The golden sun,
The planets, all the infinite host of heaven,
Are shining on the sad abodes of death,
Through the still lapse of ages. All that tread
The globe are but a handful to the tribes
That slumber in its bosom.—Take the wings
Of morning—and the Barcan desert pierce,
Or lose thyself in the continuous woods
Where rolls the Oregan, and hears no sound,
Save his own dashings—yet—the dead are there,
And millions in those solitudes, since first
The flight of years began, have laid them down
In their last sleep—the dead reign there alone.

So shalt thou rest—and what if thou shalt fall
Unheeded by the living—and no friend
Take note of thy departure? All that breathe
Will share thy destiny. The gay will laugh
When thou art gone, the solemn brood of care
Plod on, and each one as before will chase
His favorite phantom; yet all these shall leave
Their mirth and their employments, and shall
    come,
And make their bed with thee. As the long train
Of ages glide away, the sons of men,
The youth in life's green spring, and he who goes
In the full strength of years, matron, and maid,
And the sweet babe, and the gray-headed man,—
Shall one by one be gathered to thy side,
By those, who in their turn shall follow them.
So live, that when thy summons comes to join
The innumerable caravan, that moves
To that mysterious realm, where each shall take
His chamber in the silent halls of death,
Thou go not, like the quarry-slave at night,
Scourged to his dungeon, but sustained and
    soothed
By an unfaltering trust, approach thy grave,
Like one who wraps the drapery of his couch
About him, and lies down to pleasant dreams.

To a Waterfowl

  Whither, midst falling dew,
While glow the heavens with the last steps of day

Far, through their rosy depths, dost thou pursue
  Thy solitary way?

Vainly the fowler's eye
Might mark thy distant flight to do thee wrong
As, darkly seen against the crimson sky,
  Thy figure floats along.

Seek'st thou the plashy brink
Of weedy lake, or marge of river wide,
Or where the rocking billows rise and sink
  On the chafed ocean-side?

There is a Power whose care
Teaches thy way along that pathless coast—
The desert and illimitable air—
  Lone wandering, but not lost.

All day thy wings have fanned,
At that far height, the cold, thin atmosphere,
Yet stoop not, weary, to the welcome land,
  Though the dark night is near.

And soon that toil shall end;
Soon shalt thou find a summer home, and rest,
And scream among thy fellows; reeds shall bend,
  Soon, o'er thy sheltered nest.

Thou'rt gone, the abyss of heaven
Hath swallowed up thy form; yet, on my heart
Deeply has sunk the lesson thou hast given,
  And shall not soon depart.

He who, from zone to zone,
Guides through the boundless sky thy certain
  flight,
In the long way that I must tread alone,
  Will lead my steps aright.

Ralph Waldo Emerson (1803–1882)

The central figure among the Transcendentalist group of philosophers, Emerson considered himself to be first and foremost a poet, albeit one whose best work was done "for the most part in prose." His essays on nature and art have influenced writers from Whitman and Thoreau to Frost and Stevens.

Concord Hymn
*Sung at the completion of
the Concord Monument, April 19, 1836*

By the rude bridge that arched the flood,
  Their flag to April's breeze unfurled,
Here once the embattled farmers stood
  And fired the shot heard round the world.

The foe long since in silence slept,
  Alike the Conqueror silent sleeps;
And Time the ruined bridge has swept
  Down the dark stream which seaward creeps.

On this green bank, by this soft stream,
  We set to-day a votive stone,

That memory may their deed redeem,
　　When like our sires our sons are gone.

Spirit! who made those freemen dare
　　To die, or leave their children free,
Bid time and nature gently spare
　　The shaft we raise to them and Thee.

The Snow-storm

Announced by all the trumpets of the sky,
Arrives the snow, and, driving o'er the fields,
Seems nowhere to alight: the whited air
Hides hills and woods, the river, and the heaven,
And veils the farm-house at the garden's end.
The sled and traveller stopped, the courier's feet
Delayed, all friends shut out, the housemates sit
Around the radiant fireplace, enclosed
In a tumultuous privacy of storm.

　　Come see the north wind's masonry.
Out of an unseen quarry evermore
Furnished with tile, the fierce artificer
Curves his white bastions with projected roof
Round every windward stake, or tree, or door.
Speeding, the myriad-handed, his wild work
So fanciful, so savage, nought cares he
For number or proportion. Mockingly,
On coop or kennel he hangs Parian wreaths;
A swan-like form invests the hidden thorn;
Fills up the farmer's lane from wall to wall,
Maugre the farmer's sighs; and at the gate

A tapering turret overtops the work.
And when his hours are numbered, and the world
Is all his own, retiring, as he were not,
Leaves, when the sun appears, astonished Art
To mimic in slow structures, stone by stone,
Built in an age, the mad wind's night-work,
The frolic architecture of the snow.

Give All to Love

Give all to love;
Obey thy heart;
Friends, kindred, days,
Estate, good fame,
Plans, credit, and the muse;
Nothing refuse.

'Tis a brave master,
Let it have scope,
Follow it utterly,
Hope beyond hope;
High and more high,
It dives into noon,
With wing unspent,
Untold intent;
But 'tis a god,
Knows its own path,
And the outlets of the sky.

'Tis not for the mean,
It requireth courage stout,
Souls above doubt,

Valor unbending;
Such 'twill reward,
They shall return
More than they were,
And ever ascending.

Leave all for love;—
Yet, hear me, yet,
One word more thy heart behoved,
One pulse more of firm endeavor,
Keep thee to-day,
To-morrow, for ever,
Free as an Arab
Of thy beloved.
Cling with life to the maid;
But when the surprise,
Vague shadow of surmise,
Flits across her bosom young
Of a joy apart from thee,
Free be she, fancy-free,
Do not thou detain a hem,
Nor the palest rose she flung
From her summer diadem.

Though thou loved her as thyself,
As a self of purer clay,
Tho' her parting dims the day,
Stealing grace from all alive,
Heartily know,
When half-gods go,
The gods arrive.

Henry Wadsworth Longfellow (1807–1882)

The most popular American poet of the nineteenth century, Longfellow is best remembered for his long narrative poems, such as "Hiawatha" and "Evangeline." His fluid meter and his faculty for storytelling have provided an introduction to poetry for generations of readers.

The Arrow and the Song

I shot an arrow into the air,
It fell to earth, I knew not where;
For, so swiftly it flew, the sight
Could not follow it in its flight.

I breathed a song into the air,
It fell to earth, I knew not where;
For who has sight so keen and strong,
That it can follow the flight of song?

Long, long afterward, in an oak
I found the arrow, still unbroke;
And the song, from beginning to end,
I found again in the heart of a friend.

The Builders

All are architects of Fate,
    Working in these walls of Time;
Some with massive deeds and great,
    Some with ornaments of rhyme.

Nothing useless is, or low;
 Each thing in its place is best;
And what seems but idle show
 Strengthens and supports the rest.

For the structure that we raise,
 Time is with materials filled;
Our todays and yesterdays
 Are the blocks with which we build.

Truly shape and fashion these;
 Leave no yawning gaps between;
Think not, because no man sees,
 Such things will remain unseen.

In the elder days of Art,
 Builders wrought with greatest care
Each minute and unseen part;
 For the gods see everywhere.

Let us do our work as well,
 Both the unseen and the seen;
Make the house where gods may dwell
 Beautiful, entire, and clean.

Else our lives are incomplete,
 Standing in these walls of Time,
Broken stairways, where the feet
 Stumble, as they seek to climb.

Build today, then, strong and sure,
 With a firm and ample base;

And ascending and secure
   Shall tomorrow find its place.

Thus alone can we attain
   To those turrets, where the eye
Sees the world as one vast plain,
   And one boundless reach of sky.

The Children's Hour

Between the dark and the daylight,
   When the night is beginning to lower,
Comes a pause in the day's occupations
   That is known as the Children's Hour.

I hear in the chamber above me
   The patter of little feet,
The sound of a door that is opened,
   And voices soft and sweet.

From my study I see in the lamplight,
   Descending the broad hall stair,
Grave Alice, and laughing Allegra,
   And Edith with golden hair.

A whisper, and then a silence:
   Yet I know by their merry eyes
They are plotting and planning together
   To take me by surprise.

A sudden rush from the stairway,
   A sudden raid from the hall!

By three doors left unguarded
   They enter my castle wall!

They climb up into my turret
   O'er the arms and back of my chair;
If I try to escape, they surround me;
   They seem to be everywhere.

They almost devour me with kisses,
   Their arms about me entwine,
Till I think of the Bishop of Bingen
   In his Mouse-Tower on the Rhine!

Do you think, O blue-eyed banditti,
   Because you have scaled the wall,
Such an old moustache as I am
   Is not a match for you all!

I have you fast in my fortress,
   And will not let you depart,
But put you down into the dungeon
   In the round-tower of my heart.

And there will I keep you forever,
   Yes, forever and a day,
Till the walls shall crumble to ruin,
   And moulder in dust away!

The Day Is Done

The day is done, and the darkness
   Falls from the wings of Night,

As a feather is wafted downward
   From an eagle in his flight.

I see the lights of the village
   Gleam through the rain and the mist,
And a feeling of sadness comes o'er me
   That my soul cannot resist:

A feeling of sadness and longing,
   That is not akin to pain,
And resembles sorrow only
   As the mist resembles the rain.

Come, read to me some poem,
   Some simple and heartfelt lay,
That shall soothe this restless feeling,
   And banish the thoughts of day.

Not from the grand old masters,
   Not from the bards sublime,
Whose distant footsteps echo
   Through the corridors of Time.

For, like strains of martial music,
   Their mighty thoughts suggest
Life's endless toil and endeavor;
   And to-night I long for rest.

Read from some humbler poet,
   Whose songs gushed from his heart,
As showers from the clouds of summer,
   Or tears from the eyelids start;

Who, through long days of labor,
  And nights devoid of ease,
Still heard in his soul the music
  Of wonderful melodies.

Such songs have power to quiet
  The restless pulse of care,
And come like the benediction
  That follows after prayer.

Then read from the treasured volume
  The poem of thy choice,
And lend to the rhyme of the poet
  The beauty of thy voice.

And the night shall be filled with music,
  And the cares, that infest the day,
Shall fold their tents, like the Arabs,
  And as silently steal away.

Paul Revere's Ride

Listen, my children, and you shall hear
Of the midnight ride of Paul Revere,
On the eighteenth of April, in Seventy-five;
Hardly a man is now alive
Who remembers that famous day and year.

He said to his friend, "If the British march
By land or sea from the town to-night,
Hang a lantern aloft in the belfry arch
Of the North Church tower as a signal light,—
One, if by land, and two, if by sea;

And I on the opposite shore will be,
Ready to ride and spread the alarm
Through every Middlesex village and farm,
For the country folk to be up and to arm."

Then he said, "Good night!" and with muffled oar
Silently rowed to the Charlestown shore,
Just as the moon rose over the bay,
Where swinging wide of her moorings lay
The Somerset, British man-of-war;
A phantom ship, with each mast and spar
Across the moon like a prison bar,
And a huge black hulk, that was magnified
By its own reflection in the tide.

Meanwhile, his friend, through alley and street,
Wanders and watches with eager ears,
Till in the silence around him he hears
The muster of men at the barrack door,
The sound of arms, and the tramp of feet,
And the measured tread of the grenadiers,
Marching down to their boats on the shore.

Then he climbed the tower of the Old North
    Church,
By the wooden stairs, with stealthy tread,
To the belfry-chamber overhead,
And startled the pigeons from their perch
On the sombre rafters, that round him made
Masses and moving shapes of shade,—
By the trembling ladder, steep and tall,
To the highest window in the wall,

Where he paused to listen and look down
A moment on the roofs of the town,
And the moonlight flowering over all.

Beneath, in the churchyard, lay the dead,
In their night-encampment on the hill,
Wrapped in silence so deep and still
That he could hear, like a sentinel's tread,
The watchful night-wind, as it went
Creeping along from tent to tent,
And seeming to whisper, "All is well!"
A moment only he feels the spell
Of the place and the hour, and the secret dread
Of the lonely belfry and the dead;
For suddenly all his thoughts are bent
On a shadowy something far away,
Where the river widens to meet the bay,—
A line of black that bends and floats
On the rising tide, like a bridge of boats.

Meanwhile, impatient to mount and ride,
Booted and spurred, with a heavy stride
On the opposite shore walked Paul Revere.
Now he patted his horse's side,
Now gazed at the landscape far and near,
Then, impetuous, stamped the earth,
And turned and tightened his saddle-girth;
But mostly he watched with eager search
The belfry-tower of the Old North Church,
As it rose above the graves on the hill,
Lonely and spectral and sombre and still.

And lo! as he looks, on the belfry's height
A glimmer, and then a gleam of light!
He springs to the saddle, the bridle he turns,
But lingers and gazes, till full on his sight
A second lamp in the belfry burns!

A hurry of hoofs in a village street,
A shape in the moonlight, a bulk in the dark,
And beneath, from the pebbles, in passing, a spark
Struck out by a steed flying fearless and fleet:
That was all! And yet, through the gloom and
    the light,
The fate of a nation was riding that night;
And the spark struck out by that steed, in his flight,
Kindled the land into flame with its heat.

He has left the village and mounted the steep,
And beneath him, tranquil and broad and deep,
Is the Mystic, meeting the ocean tides;
And under the alders that skirt its edge,
Now soft on the sand, now loud on the ledge,
Is heard the tramp of his steed as he rides.

It was twelve by the village clock,
When he crossed the bridge into Medford town.
He heard the crowing of the cock,
And the barking of the farmer's dog,
And felt the damp of the river fog,
That rises after the sun goes down.

It was one by the village clock,
When he galloped into Lexington.

He saw the gilded weathercock
Swim in the moonlight as he passed,
And the meeting-house windows, blank and bare,
Gaze at him with a spectral glare,
As if they already stood aghast
At the bloody work they would look upon.

It was two by the village clock,
When he came to the bridge in Concord town.
He heard the bleating of the flock,
And the twitter of the birds among the trees,
And felt the breath of the morning breeze
Blowing over the meadows brown.
And one was safe and asleep in his bed
Who at the bridge would be first to fall,
Who that day would be lying dead,
Pierced by a British musket-ball.

You know the rest. In the books you have read,
How the British Regulars fired and fled,—
How the farmers gave them ball for ball,
From behind each fence and farm-yard wall,
Chasing the red-coats down the lane,
Then crossing the fields to emerge again
Under the trees at the turn of the road,
And only pausing to fire and load.

So through the night rode Paul Revere;
And so through the night went his cry of alarm
To every Middlesex village and farm,—

A cry of defiance and not of fear,
A voice in the darkness, a knock at the door,
And a word that shall echo forevermore!
For, borne on the night-wind of the Past,
Through all our history, to the last,
In the hour of darkness and peril and need,
The people will waken and listen to hear
The hurrying hoof-beats of that steed,
And the midnight message of Paul Revere.

The Cross of Snow

In the long, sleepless watches of the night
  A gentle face—the face of one long dead—
  Looks at me from the wall, where round its
    head
  The night-lamp casts a halo of pale light.
Here in this room she died; and soul more white
  Never through martyrdom of fire was led
  To its repose; nor can in books be read
  The legend of a life more benedight.
There is a mountain in the distant West
  That, sun-defying, in its deep ravines
  Displays a cross of snow upon its side.
Such is the cross I wear upon my breast
  These eighteen years, through all the
    changing scenes
  And seasons, changeless since the day she died.

John Greenleaf Whittier (1807–1892)

A Quaker, Whittier was an ardent abolitionist and one of the most prolific and popular American poets of his time.

Forgiveness

My heart was heavy, for its trust had been
    Abused, its kindness answered with foul wrong;
So, turning gloomily from my fellow-men,
    One summer Sabbath day I strolled among
The green mounds of the village burial-place;
    Where, pondering how all human love and hate
    Find one sad level; and how, soon or late,
Wronged and wrongdoer, each with meekened face,
    And cold hands folded over a still heart,
Pass the green threshold of our common grave,
    Whither all footsteps tend, whence none depart,
Awed for myself, and pitying my race,
Our common sorrow, like a mighty wave,
Swept all my pride away, and trembling I forgave!

Godspeed

Outbound, your bark awaits you. Were I one
    Whose prayer availeth much, my wish should be
    Your favoring trade-wind and consenting sea.
By sail or steed was never love outrun,
And, here or there, love follows her in whom
    All graces and sweet charities unite,

The old Greek beauty set in holier light;
And her for whom New England's byways bloom,
Who walks among us welcome as the Spring,
   Calling up blossoms where her light feet stray.
   God keep you both, make beautiful your way,
Comfort, console, and bless; and safely bring,
Ere yet I make upon a vaster sea
The unreturning voyage, my friends to me.

Edgar Allan Poe (1809–1849)

One of America's greatest writers of horror and mystery fiction, Poe was also an innovative poet. His highly evocative verse stresses the musical nature of the poetic form.

Alone

From childhood's hour I have not been
As others were—I have not seen
As others saw—I could not bring
My passions from a common spring.
From the same source I have not taken
My sorrow; I could not awaken
My heart to joy at the same tone;
And all I lov'd, *I* lov'd alone.
Then—in my childhood—in the dawn
Of a most stormy life—was drawn
From ev'ry depth of good and ill
The mystery which binds me still:
From the torrent, or the fountain,

From the red cliff of the mountain,
From the sun that 'round me roll'd
In its autumn tint of gold—
From the lightning in the sky
As it pass'd me flying by—
From the thunder and the storm,
And the cloud that took the form
(When the rest of Heaven was blue)
Of a demon in my view.

Annabel Lee

It was many and many a year ago,
  In a kingdom by the sea,
That a maiden there lived whom you may know
  By the name of Annabel Lee;
And this maiden she lived with no other thought
  Than to love and be loved by me.

I was a child and *she* was a child,
  In this kingdom by the sea:
But we loved with a love that was more than love—
  I and my Annabel Lee—
With a love that the wingèd seraphs of Heaven
  Coveted her and me.

And this was the reason that, long ago,
  In this kingdom by the sea,
A wind blew out of a cloud, chilling
  My beautiful Annabel Lee;
So that her high-born kinsmen came
  And bore her away from me,

To shut her up in a sepulchre
   In this kingdom by the sea.

The angels, not half so happy in heaven,
   Went envying her and me—
Yes!—that was the reason (as all men know,
   In this kingdom by the sea)
That the wind came out of the cloud by night,
   Chilling and killing my Annabel Lee.

But our love it was stronger by far than the love
   Of those who were older than we—
   Of many far wiser than we—
And neither the angels in heaven above
   Nor the demons down under the sea,
Can ever dissever my soul from the soul
   Of the beautiful Annabel Lee:

For the moon never beams, without bringing me
   dreams
   Of the beautiful Annabel Lee;
And the stars never rise, but I feel the bright eyes
   Of the beautiful Annabel Lee;
And so, all the night-tide, I lie down by the side
Of my darling—my darling—my life and my bride,
   In her sepulchre there by the sea,
   In her tomb by the sounding sea.

The Conqueror Worm

   Lo! 'tis a gala night
      Within the lonesome latter years!

An angel throng, bewinged, bedight
   In veils, and drowned in tears,
Sit in a theatre, to see
   A play of hopes and fears,
While the orchestra breathes fitfully
   The music of the spheres.

Mimes, in the form of God on high,
   Mutter and mumble low,
And hither and thither fly—
   Mere puppets they, who come and go
At bidding of vast formless things
   That shift the scenery to and fro,
Flapping from out their Condor wings
   Invisible Woe!

That motley drama—oh, be sure
   It shall not be forgot!
With its Phantom chased for evermore,
   By a crowd that seize it not,
Through a circle that ever returneth in
   To the self-same spot,
And much of Madness, and more of Sin,
   And Horror the soul of the plot.

But see, amid the mimic rout
   A crawling shape intrude!
A blood-red thing that writhes from out
   The scenic solitude!
It writhes!—it writhes!—with mortal pangs
   The mimes become its food,

And the angels sob at vermin fangs
   In human gore imbued.

Out—out are the lights—out all!
   And, over each quivering form,
The curtain, a funeral pall,
   Comes down with the rush of a storm,
And the angels, all pallid and wan,
   Uprising, unveiling, affirm
That the play is the tragedy "Man,"
   And its hero the Conqueror Worm.

The Raven

Once upon a midnight dreary, while I pondered,
   weak and weary,
Over many a quaint and curious volume of for-
   gotten lore—
While I nodded, nearly napping, suddenly there
   came a tapping,
As of some one gently rapping, rapping at my
   chamber door.
"'T is some visitor," I muttered, "tapping at my
   chamber door—
   Only this, and nothing more."

Ah, distinctly I remember it was in the bleak
   December;
And each separate dying ember wrought its
   ghost upon the floor.
Eagerly I wished the morrow;—vainly I had
   sought to borrow

From my books surcease of sorrow—sorrow for
the lost Lenore—
For the rare and radiant maiden whom the an-
gels name Lenore—
Nameless *here* for evermore.

And the silken, sad, uncertain rustling of each
purple curtain
Thrilled me—filled me with fantastic terrors
never felt before;
So that now, to still the beating of my heart, I
stood repeating
"'T is some visitor entreating entrance at my
chamber door—
Some late visitor entreating entrance at my
chamber door;—
This it is and nothing more."

Presently my soul grew stronger; hesitating then
no longer,
"Sir," said I, "or Madam, truly your forgiveness
I implore;
But the fact is I was napping, and so gently you
came rapping,
And so faintly you came tapping, tapping at my
chamber door,
That I scarce was sure I heard you"—here I
opened wide the door;—
Darkness there, and nothing more.

Deep into the darkness peering, long I stood
  there wondering, fearing,
Doubting, dreaming dreams no mortal ever
  dared to dream before;
But the silence was unbroken, and the stillness
  gave no token,
And the only word there spoken was the whis-
  pered word, "Lenore!"
This I whispered, and an echo murmured back
  the word "Lenore!"
    Merely this, and nothing more.

Back into the chamber turning, all my soul
  within me burning,
Soon again I heard a tapping, somewhat louder
  than before.
"Surely," said I, "surely, that is something at my
  window lattice;
Let me see, then, what thereat is, and this mys-
  tery explore;
Let my heart be still a moment and this mystery
  explore;—
    'T is the wind, and nothing more."

Open here I flung the shutter, when, with many
  a flirt and flutter,
In there stepped a stately raven, of the saintly
  days of yore.
Not the least obeisance made he; not a minute
  stopped or stayed he;

But, with mien of lord or lady, perched above
    my chamber door;—
Perched upon a bust of Pallas just above my
    chamber door—
      Perched, and sat, and nothing more.

Then this ebony bird beguiling my sad fancy
    into smiling,
By the grave and stern decorum of the counte-
    nance it wore,
"Though thy crest be shorn and shaven, thou," I
    said, "art sure no craven,
Ghastly, grim, and ancient Raven, wandering
    from the Nightly shore,
Tell me what thy lordly name is on the Night's
    Plutonian shore."
      Quoth the Raven, "Nevermore."

Much I marvelled this ungainly fowl to hear dis-
    course so plainly,
Though its answer little meaning—little rele-
    vancy bore;
For we cannot help agreeing that no living
    human being
Ever yet was blessed with seeing bird above his
    chamber door—
Bird or beast upon the sculptured bust above his
    chamber door,
      With such name as "Nevermore."

But the Raven, sitting lonely on the placid bust,
   spoke only
That one word, as if his soul in that one word he
   did outpour.
Nothing farther then he uttered—not a feather
   then he fluttered—
Till I scarcely more than muttered, "Other
   friends have flown before—
On the morrow *he* will leave me, as my hopes
   have flown before."
      Then the bird said, "Nevermore."

Startled at the stillness broken by reply so aptly
   spoken,
"Doubtless," said I, "what it utters is its only
   stock and store,
Caught from some unhappy master, whom un-
   merciful Disaster
Followed fast and followed faster till his songs
   one burden bore—
Till the dirges of his Hope that melancholy bur-
   den bore
      Of 'Never-nevermore.'"

But the Raven still beguiling all my fancy into
   smiling,
Straight I wheeled a cushioned seat in front of
   bird, and bust and door;
Then, upon the velvet sinking, I betook myself
   to linking

Fancy unto fancy, thinking what this ominous
    bird of yore—
What this grim, ungainly, ghastly, gaunt, and
    ominous bird of yore
        Meant in croaking "Nevermore."

This I sat engaged in guessing, but no syllable
    expressing
To the fowl whose fiery eyes now burned into
    my bosom's core;
This and more I sat divining, with my head at
    ease reclining
On the cushion's velvet lining that the lamp-
    light gloated o'er,
But whose velvet violet lining with the lamp-
    light gloating o'er,
        She shall press, ah, nevermore!

Then, methought, the air grew denser, perfumed
    from an unseen censer
Swung by Seraphim whose foot-falls tinkled on
    the tufted floor.
"Wretch," I cried, "thy God hath lent thee—by
    these angels he hath sent thee
Respite—respite and nepenthe from thy memo-
    ries of Lenore;
Quaff, oh quaff this kind nepenthe and forget
    this lost Lenore!"
        Quoth the Raven, "Nevermore."

"Prophet!" said I, "thing of evil!—prophet still,
    if bird or devil!—
Whether Tempter sent, or whether tempest
    tossed thee here ashore,
Desolate yet all undaunted, on this desert land
    enchanted—
On this home by Horror haunted—tell me truly,
    I implore—
Is there—*is* there balm in Gilead?—tell me—tell
    me, I implore!"
        Quoth the Raven, "Nevermore."

"Prophet!" said I, "thing of evil!—prophet still,
    if bird or devil!
By that Heaven that bends above us—by that
    God we both adore—
Tell this soul with sorrow laden if, within the
    distant Aidenn,
It shall clasp a sainted maiden whom the angels
    name Lenore—
Clasp a rare and radiant maiden whom the an-
    gels name Lenore."
        Quoth the Raven, "Nevermore."

"Be that word our sign of parting, bird or
    fiend!" I shrieked, upstarting—
"Get thee back into the tempest and the Night's
    Plutonian shore!
Leave no black plume as a token of that lie thy
    soul hath spoken!

Leave my loneliness unbroken!—quit the bust
    above my door!
Take thy beak from out my heart, and take thy
    form from off my door!"
      Quoth the Raven, "Nevermore."

And the Raven, never flitting, still is sitting, *still*
    is sitting
On the pallid bust of Pallas just above my cham-
    ber door;
And his eyes have all the seeming of a demon's
    that is dreaming,
And the lamp-light o'er him streaming throws
    his shadow on the floor;
And my soul from out that shadow that lies
    floating on the floor
      Shall be lifted—nevermore!

To Helen

Helen, thy beauty is to me
    Like those Nicéan barks of yore,
That gently, o'er a perfumed sea,
    The weary, way-worn wanderer bore
    To his own native shore.

On desperate seas long wont to roam,
    Thy hyacinth hair, thy classic face,
Thy Naiad airs have brought me home
    To the glory that was Greece,
    And the grandeur that was Rome.

Lo! in yon brilliant window-niche
　　How statue-like I see thee stand,
The agate lamp within thy hand!
　　Ah, Psyche, from the regions which
　　Are Holy-Land!

Oliver Wendell Holmes, Sr. (1809–1894)

A professor of anatomy, Holmes won renown as an occasional poet and an essayist. "Old Ironsides"—written to protest the dismantling of the frigate *Constitution*—made the preservation of the ship a national cause.

Old Ironsides

Ay, tear her tattered ensign down!
　　Long has it waved on high,
And many an eye has danced to see
　　That banner in the sky;
Beneath it rung the battle shout,
　　And burst the cannon's roar;—
The meteor of the ocean air
　　Shall sweep the clouds no more!

Her deck, once red with heroes' blood,
　　Where knelt the vanquished foe,
When winds were hurrying o'er the flood,
　　And waves were white below,
No more shall feel the victor's tread,
　　Or know the conquered knee;—

The harpies of the shore shall pluck
    The eagle of the sea!

O better that her shattered hulk
    Should sink beneath the wave;
Her thunders shook the mighty deep,
    And there should be her grave;
Nail to the mast her holy flag,
    Set every threadbare sail,
And give her to the god of storms,—
    The lightning and the gale!

The Deacon's Masterpiece
or, The Wonderful 'One-Hoss Shay'

A Logical Story

Have you heard of the wonderful one-hoss shay,
That was built in such a logical way
It ran a hundred years to a day,
And then, of a sudden, it—ah, but stay,
I'll tell you what happened without delay,
Scaring the parson into fits,
Frightening people out of their wits,—
Have you ever heard of that, I say?

Seventeen hundred and fifty-five.
Georgius Secundus was then alive,—
Snuffy old drone from the German hive.
That was the year when Lisbon-town
Saw the earth open and gulp her down,
And Braddock's army was done so brown,

Left without a scalp to its crown.
It was on the terrible Earthquake-day
That the Deacon finished the one-hoss shay.

Now in building of chaises, I tell you what,
There is always *somewhere* a weakest spot,—
In hub, tire, felloe, in spring or thill,
In panel, or crossbar, or floor, or sill,
In screw, bolt, thoroughbrace,—lurking still,
Find it somewhere you must and will,—
Above or below, or within or without,—
And that's the reason, beyond a doubt,
That a chaise *breaks down,* but doesn't *wear out.*

But the Deacon swore (as Deacons do,
With an 'I dew vum,' or an 'I tell *yeou*')
He would build one shay to beat the taown
'n' the keounty 'n' all the kentry raoun';
It should be so built that it *couldn'* break daown:
'Fur,' said the Deacon, ''t 's mighty plain
Thut the weakes' place mus' stan' the strain;
'n' the way t' fix it, uz I maintain,
        Is only jest
T' make that place uz strong uz the rest.'

So the Deacon inquired of the village folk
Where he could find the strongest oak,
That couldn't be split nor bent nor broke,—
That was for spokes and floor and sills;
He sent for lancewood to make the thills;
The crossbars were ash, from the straightest trees,

The panels of white-wood, that cuts like cheese,
But lasts like iron for things like these;
The hubs of logs from the 'Settler's ellum,'—
Last of its timber,—they couldn't sell 'em,
Never an axe had seen their chips,
And the wedges flew from between their lips,
Their blunt ends frizzled like celery-tips;
Step and prop-iron, bolt and screw,
Spring, tire, axle, and linchpin too,
Steel of the finest, bright and blue;
Thoroughbrace bison-skin, thick and wide;
Boot, top, dasher, from tough old hide
Found in the pit when the tanner died.
That was the way he 'put her through.'
'There!' said the Deacon, 'naow she'll dew!'

Do! I tell you, I rather guess
She was a wonder, and nothing less!
Colts grew horses, beards turned gray,
Deacon and deaconess dropped away,
Children and grandchildren—where were they?
But there stood the stout old one-hoss shay
As fresh as on Lisbon-earthquake-day!

Eighteen hundred;—it came and found
The Deacon's masterpiece strong and sound.
Eighteen hundred increased by ten;—
'Hahnsum kerridge' they called it then.
Eighteen hundred and twenty came;—
Running as usual; much the same.

Thirty and forty at last arrive,
And then come fifty, and fifty-five.

Little of all we value here
Wakes on the morn of its hundredth year
Without both feeling and looking queer.
In fact, there's nothing that keeps its youth,
So far as I know, but a tree and truth.
(This is a moral that runs at large;
Take it.—You're welcome.—No extra charge.)

First of November,—the Earthquake-day,—
There are traces of age in the one-hoss shay,
A general flavor of mild decay,
But nothing local, as one may say.
There couldn't be,—for the Deacon's art
Had made it so like in every part
That there wasn't a chance for one to start.
For the wheels were just as strong as the thills,
And the floor was just as strong as the sills,
And the panels just as strong as the floor,
And the whipple-tree neither less nor more,
And the back-crossbar as strong as the fore,
And spring and axle and hub *encore.*
And yet, *as a whole,* it is past a doubt
In another hour it will be *worn out!*

First of November, 'Fifty-five!
This morning the parson takes a drive.
Now, small boys, get out of the way!
Here comes the wonderful one-hoss shay,

Drawn by a rat-tailed, ewe-necked bay.
'Huddup!' said the parson.—Off went they.
The parson was working his Sunday's text,—
Had got to *fifthly,* and stopped perplexed
At what the—Moses—was coming next.
All at once the horse stood still,
Close by the meet'n'-house on the hill.
First a shiver, and then a thrill,
Then something decidedly like a spill,—
And the parson was sitting upon a rock,
At half past nine by the meet'n'-house clock,—
Just the hour of the Earthquake shock!
What do you think the parson found,
When he got up and stared around?
The poor old chaise in a heap or mound,
As if it had been to the mill and ground!
You see, of course, if you're not a dunce,
How it went to pieces all at once,—
All at once, and nothing first,—
Just as bubbles do when they burst.

End of the wonderful one-hoss shay.
Logic is logic. That's all I say.

Jones Very (1813–1880)

Born in Salem, Massachusetts, Very was a reli-
gious mystic whose poetry revealed a profound
submission to the will of God. His poems on

religious themes have often been compared to
the verse of George Herbert and other seven-
teenth-century metaphysical poets.

The Cottage

The house my earthly parent left
My heavenly parent still throws down,
For 't is of air and sun bereft,
Nor stars its roof with beauty crown.

He gave it me, yet gave it not
As one whose gifts are wise and good;
'T was but a poor and clay-built cot,
And for a time the storms withstood.

But lengthening years and frequent rain
O'ercame its strength: it tottered, fell,
And left me homeless here again,—
And where to go I could not tell.

But soon the light and open air
Received me as a wandering child,
And I soon thought their house more fair,
And all my grief their love beguiled.

Mine was the grove, the pleasant field
Where dwelt the flowers I daily trod;
And there beside them, too, I kneeled
And called their friend, my Father, God.

Henry David Thoreau (1817–1862)

Best known for such prose works as *Walden* and *A Week on the Concord and Merrimack Rivers,* Thoreau expressed his philosophy of salvation through nature in his poetry as well, as in the beautifully lyrical selection reprinted here.

Winter Memories

Within the circuit of this plodding life
There enter moments of an azure hue,
Untarnished fair as is the violet
Or anemone, when the spring strews them
By some meandering rivulet, which make
The best philosophy untrue that aims
But to console man for his grievances.
I have remembered when the winter came,
High in my chamber in the frosty nights,
When in the still light of the cheerful moon,
On every twig and rail and jutting spout,
The icy spears were adding to their length
Against the arrows of the coming sun,
How in the shimmering noon of summer past
Some unrecorded beam slanted across
The upland pastures where the Johnswort grew;
Or heard, amid the verdure of my mind,
The bee's long smothered hum, on the blue flag
Loitering amidst the mead; or busy rill,
Which now through all its course stands still
   and dumb

Its own memorial,—purling at its play
Along the slopes, and through the meadows next,
Until its youthful sound was hushed at last
In the staid current of the lowland stream;
Or seen the furrows shine but late upturned,
And where the fieldfare followed in the rear,
When all the fields around lay bound and hoar
Beneath a thick integument of snow.
So by God's cheap economy made rich
To go upon my winter's task again.

Herman Melville (1819–1891)

Melville only began to write poetry seriously in the 1860s, well after the publication of his more famous novels, including *Moby-Dick* (1851). Neglected for many years, his poems on the Civil War are now thought to rival those of his contemporary, Walt Whitman.

Misgivings
(1860)

When ocean-clouds over inland hills
   Sweep storming in late autumn brown,
And horror the sodden valley fills,
   And the spire falls crashing in the town,
I muse upon my country's ills—
The tempest bursting from the waste of Time
On the world's fairest hope linked with man's
   foulest crime.

Nature's dark side is heeded now—
   (Ah! optimist-cheer disheartened flown)—
A child may read the moody brow
   Of yon black mountain lone.
With shouts the torrents down the gorges go,
And storms are formed behind the storm we
   feel:
The hemlock shakes in the rafter, the oak in the
   driving keel.

Julia Ward Howe (1819–1910)

Born into a well-to-do family in New York City,
Julia Ward Howe was prominent during the Civil
War, thanks to her poem "Battle Hymn of the
Republic." Sung to the tune of "John Brown's
Body," the famous poem, written in 1861 while
visiting an army camp, became the war song of
the Union army. *Passion Flowers* (1854), *Words
for the Hour* (1857), and *Later Lyrics* (1866) are
some of Howe's books of poems.

Battle Hymn of the Republic

Mine eyes have seen the glory of the coming of
   the Lord:
He is trampling out the vintage where the grapes
   of wrath are stored;
He hath loosed the fateful lightning of his terri-
   ble swift sword:
     His truth is marching on.

I have seen Him in the watch-fires of a hundred
   circling camps;
They have builded Him an altar in the evening
   dews and damps;
I can read His righteous sentence by the dim
   and flaring lamps.
      His day is marching on.

I have read a fiery gospel, writ in burnished rows
   of steel:
"As ye deal with my contemners, so with you my
   grace shall deal;
Let the Hero, born of woman, crush the serpent
   with his heel,
      Since God is marching on."

He has sounded forth the trumpet that shall
   never call retreat;
He is sifting out the hearts of men before his
   judgment-seat:
Oh! be swift, my soul, to answer Him! be jubi-
   lant, my feet!
      Our God is marching on.

In the beauty of the lilies Christ was born across
   the sea,
With a glory in his bosom that transfigures you
   and me:
As he died to make men holy, let us die to make
   men free,
      While God is marching on.

Walt Whitman (1819–1892)

Writing in long, loose lines and a self-described "barbaric yawp," Whitman introduced to American poetry a democratic, all-encompassing vision and a freedom of style that liberated the form from its traditional constraints.

I Hear America Singing

I hear America singing, the varied carols I hear,
Those of mechanics, each one singing his as it
    should be blithe and strong,
The carpenter singing his as he measures his
    plank or beam,
The mason singing his as he makes ready for
    work, or leaves off work,
The boatman singing what belongs to him in his
    boat, the deck-hand singing on the steamboat
    deck,
The shoemaker singing as he sits on his bench,
    the hatter singing as he stands,
The wood-cutter's song, the ploughboy's on his
    way in the morning, or at noon intermission
    or at sundown,
The delicious singing of the mother, or of the
    young wife at work, or of the girl sewing or
    washing,
Each singing what belongs to him or her and to
    none else,

The day what belongs to the day—at night the
   party of young fellows, robust, friendly,
Singing with open mouths their strong melodi-
   ous songs.

I Sit and Look Out

I sit and look out upon all the sorrows of the
   world, and upon all oppression and shame,
I hear secret convulsive sobs from young men at
   anguish with themselves, remorseful after
   deeds done,
I see in low life the mother misused by her chil-
   dren, dying, neglected, gaunt, desperate,
I see the wife misused by her husband, I see the
   treacherous seducer of young women,
I mark the ranklings of jealousy and unrequited
   love attempted to be hid, I see these sights on
   the earth,
I see the workings of battle, pestilence, tyranny,
   I see martyrs and prisoners,
I observe a famine at sea, I observe the sailors
   casting lots who shall be kill'd to preserve the
   lives of the rest,
I observe the slights and degradations cast by
   arrogant persons upon laborers, the poor, and
   upon negroes, and the like;
All these—all the meanness and agony without
   end I sitting look out upon,
See, hear, and am silent.

Miracles

Why, who makes much of a miracle?
As to me I know of nothing else but miracles,
Whether I walk the streets of Manhattan,
Or dart my sight over the roofs of houses to-
    ward the sky,
Or wade with naked feet along the beach just in
    the edge of the water,
Or stand under trees in the woods,
Or talk by day with any one I love, or sleep in
    the bed at night with any one I love,
Or sit at table at dinner with the rest,
Or look at strangers opposite me riding in the
    car,
Or watch honey-bees busy around the hive of a
    summer forenoon,
Or animals feeding in the fields,
Or birds, or the wonderfulness of insects in the
    air,
Or the wonderfulness of the sundown, or of
    stars shining so quiet and bright,
Or the exquisite delicate thin curve of the new
    moon in spring;
These with the rest, one and all, are to me mira-
    cles,
The whole referring, yet each distinct and in its
    place.

To me every hour of the light and dark is a mir-
    acle,

Every cubic inch of space is a miracle,
Every square yard of the surface of the earth is
  spread with the same,
Every foot of the interior swarms with the same.

To me the sea is a continual miracle,
The fishes that swim—the rocks—the motion of
  the waves—the ships with men in them,
What stranger miracles are there?

A Noiseless Patient Spider

A noiseless patient spider,
I mark'd where on a little promontory it stood
  isolated,
Mark'd how to explore the vacant vast sur-
  rounding,
It launch'd forth filament, filament, filament,
  out of itself,
Ever unreeling them, ever tirelessly speeding
  them.

And you O my soul where you stand,
Surrounded, detached, in measureless oceans of
  space,
Ceaselessly musing, venturing, throwing, seek-
  ing the spheres to connect them,
Till the bridge you will need be form'd, till the
  ductile anchor hold,
Till the gossamer thread you fling catch some-
  where, O my soul.

O Captain! My Captain!

O Captain! my Captain! our fearful trip is done,
The ship has weather'd every rack, the prize we
    sought is won,
The port is near, the bells I hear, the people all
    exulting,
While follow eyes the steady keel, the vessel grim
    and daring;
      But O heart! heart! heart!
        O the bleeding drops of red,
          Where on the deck my Captain lies,
          Fallen cold and dead.

O Captain! my Captain! rise up and hear the
    bells;
Rise up—for you the flag is flung—for you the
    bugle trills,
For you bouquets and ribbon'd wreaths—for
    you the shores a-crowding,
For you they call, the swaying mass, their eager
    faces turning;
      Here Captain! dear father!
        This arm beneath your head!
          It is some dream that on the deck,
          You've fallen cold and dead.

My Captain does not answer, his lips are pale
    and still,
My father does not feel my arm, he has no pulse
    nor will,

The ship is anchor'd safe and sound, its voyage
  closed and done,
From fearful trip the victor ship comes in with
  object won;
     Exult O shores, and ring O bells!
      But I with mournful tread,
       Walk the deck my Captain lies,
        Fallen cold and dead.

From Song of Myself*

1

I celebrate myself, and sing myself,
And what I assume you shall assume,
For every atom belonging to me as good be-
  longs to you.

I loafe and invite my soul,
I lean and loafe at my ease observing a spear of
  summer grass.
My tongue, every atom of my blood, form'd
  from this soil, this air,
Born here of parents born here from parents the
  same, and their parents the same.
I, now thirty-seven years old in perfect health
  begin,
Hoping to cease not till death.

---

*The first and last stanzas of "Song of Myself" are ex-
cerpted here.

Creeds and schools in abeyance,
Retiring back a while sufficed at what they are,
  but never forgotten,
I harbor for good or bad, I permit to speak at
  every hazard,
Nature without check with original energy.

* * *

52

The spotted hawk swoops by and accuses me, he
  complains of my gab and my loitering.

I too am not a bit tamed, I too am untranslat-
  able,
I sound my barbaric yawp over the roofs of the
  world.

The last scud of day holds back for me,
It flings my likeness after the rest and true as
  any on the shadow'd wilds,
It coaxes me to the vapor and the dusk.

I depart as air, I shake my white locks at the run-
  away sun,
I effuse my flesh in eddies, and drift it in lacy
  jags.

I bequeath myself to the dirt to grow from the
  grass I love,
If you want me again look for me under your
  boot-soles.

You will hardly know who I am or what I mean,
But I shall be good health to you nevertheless,
And filter and fibre your blood.

Failing to fetch me at first keep encouraged,
Missing me one place search another,
I stop somewhere waiting for you.

When I Heard the Learn'd Astronomer

When I heard the learn'd astronomer,
When the proofs, the figures, were ranged in
    columns before me,
When I was shown the charts and diagrams, to
    add, divide, and measure them,
When I sitting heard the astronomer where he
    lectured with much applause in the lecture-
    room,
How soon unaccountable I became tired and sick,
Till rising and gliding out I wander'd off by my-
    self,
In the mystical moist night-air, and from time to
    time,
Look'd up in perfect silence at the stars.

Frances E. W. Harper (1825–1911)

A prolific author in almost every literary genre,
Frances Harper used her writing as a vehicle for
advocating racial equality (she was herself the
daughter of freed slaves) and women's rights.

Bury Me in a Free Land

Make me a grave where'er you will,
In a lowly plain, or a lofty hill,
Make it among earth's humblest graves,
But not in a land where men are slaves.

I could not rest if around my grave
I heard the steps of a trembling slave:
His shadow above my silent tomb
Would make it a place of fearful gloom.

I could not rest if I heard the tread
Of a coffle gang to the shambles led,
And the mother's shriek of wild despair
Rise like a curse on the trembling air.

I could not sleep if I saw the lash
Drinking her blood at each fearful gash,
And I saw her babes torn from her breast,
Like trembling doves from their parent nest.

I'd shudder and start if I heard the bay
Of blood-hounds seizing their human prey,
And I heard the captive plead in vain
As they bound afresh his galling chain.

If I saw young girls from their mother's arms
Bartered and sold for their youthful charms,
My eye would flash with a mournful flame,
My death-paled cheek grow red with shame.

I would sleep, dear friends, where bloated might
Can rob no man of his dearest right;
My rest shall be calm in any grave
Where none can call his brother a slave.

I ask no monument, proud and high,
To arrest the gaze of the passers-by;
All that my yearning spirit craves,
Is bury me not in a land of slaves.

Songs for the People

Let me make the songs for the people,
　　Songs for the old and young;
Songs to stir like a battle-cry
　　Wherever they are sung.

Not for the clashing of sabres,
　　For carnage nor for strife;
But songs to thrill the hearts of men
　　With more abundant life.

Let me make the songs for the weary,
　　Amid life's fever and fret,
Till hearts shall relax their tension,
　　And careworn brows forget.

Let me sing for little children,
　　Before their footsteps stray,
Sweet anthems of love and duty,
　　To float o'er life's highway.

I would sing for the poor and aged,
　When shadows dim their sight;
Of the bright and restful mansions,
　Where there shall be no night.

Our world, so worn and weary,
　Needs music, pure and strong,
To hush the jangle and discords
　Of sorrow, pain, and wrong.

Music to soothe all its sorrow,
　Till war and crime shall cease;
And the hearts of men grown tender
　Girdle the world with peace.

Emily Dickinson (1830–1886)

A near-recluse for most of her life, Emily Dickinson was highly imaginative in her use of language and syntax, and concentrated on such themes as death, loss, and beauty with a disarming casualness. Though Dickinson is today regarded as one of America's greatest poets, fewer than ten of her poems were published during her lifetime.

'Because I could not stop for Death'

Because I could not stop for Death,
He kindly stopped for me;
The carriage held but just ourselves
And Immortality.

We slowly drove, he knew no haste,
And I had put away
My labor, and my leisure too,
For his civility.

We passed the school where children played,
Their lessons scarcely done;
We passed the fields of gazing grain,
We passed the setting sun.

We paused before a house that seemed
A swelling of the ground;
The roof was scarcely visible,
The cornice but a mound.

Since then 't is centuries; but each
Feels shorter than the day
I first surmised the horses' heads
Were toward eternity.

'Death sets a thing significant'

Death sets a thing significant
The eye had hurried by,
Except a perished creature
Entreat us tenderly

To ponder little workmanships
In crayon or in wool,
With "This was last her fingers did,"
Industrious until

The thimble weighed too heavy,
The stitches stopped themselves,
And then 't was put among the dust
Upon the closet shelves.

A book I have, a friend gave,
Whose pencil, here and there,
Had notched the place that pleased him,—
At rest his fingers are.

Now, when I read, I read not,
For interrupting tears
Obliterate the etchings
Too costly for repairs.

'Hope is the thing with feathers'

Hope is the thing with feathers
That perches in the soul,
And sings the tune without the words,
And never stops at all,

And sweetest in the gale is heard;
And sore must be the storm
That could abash the little bird
That kept so many warm.

I've heard it in the chillest land,
And on the strangest sea;
Yet, never, in extremity,
It asked a crumb of me.

'I died for beauty'

I died for beauty, but was scarce
Adjusted in the tomb,
When one who died for truth was lain
In an adjoining room.

He questioned softly why I failed?
"For beauty," I replied.
"And I for truth,—the two are one;
We brethren are," he said.

And so, as kinsmen met a night,
We talked between the rooms,
Until the moss had reached our lips,
And covered up our names.

'If I can stop one heart from breaking'

If I can stop one heart from breaking,
I shall not live in vain;
If I can ease one life the aching,
Or cool one pain,
Or help one fainting robin
Unto his nest again,
I shall not live in vain.

'I'm nobody! Who are you?'

I'm nobody! Who are you?
Are you nobody, too?
Then there's a pair of us—don't tell!
They'd banish us, you know.

How dreary to be somebody!
How public, like a frog
To tell your name the livelong day
To an admiring bog!

'My life closed twice before its close'

My life closed twice before its close;
    It yet remains to see
If Immortality unveil
    A third event to me,

So huge, so hopeless to conceive,
    As these that twice befell.
Parting is all we know of heaven,
    And all we need of hell.

'Success is counted sweetest'

Success is counted sweetest
By those who ne'er succeed.
To comprehend a nectar
Requires sorest need.

Not one of all the purple host
Who took the flag today
Can tell the definition,
So clear, of victory

As he, defeated, dying,
On whose forbidden ear
The distant strains of triumph
Break, agonized and clear.

'There is no frigate like a book'

There is no frigate like a book
   To take us lands away,
Nor any coursers like a page
   Of prancing poetry.
This traverse may the poorest take
   Without oppress of toll;
How frugal is the chariot
   That bears a human soul!

'This is my letter to the world'

This is my letter to the world,
   That never wrote to me,—
The simple news that Nature told,
   With tender majesty.

Her message is committed
   To hands I cannot see;
For love of her, sweet countrymen,
   Judge tenderly of me!

James Whitcomb Riley (1849–1916)

"The Hoosier Poet," particularly popular for the poems in the dialect of his home state, Indiana.

Silence

Thousands and thousands of hushed years ago,
   Out on the edge of Chaos, all alone
   I stood on peaks of vapor, high upthrown

Above a sea that knew nor ebb nor flow,
Nor any motion won of winds that blow,
 Nor any sound of watery wail or moan,
 Nor lisp of wave, nor wandering undertone
Of any tide lost in the night below.
So still it was, I mind me, as I laid
 My thirsty ear against mine own faint sigh
To drink of that, I sipped it, half afraid
 'Twas but the ghost of a dead voice spilled by
The one starved star that tottered through the
  shade
 And came tiptoeing toward me down the sky.

Emma Lazarus (1849–1887)

A poet, philanthropist, and advocate of Jewish causes, Emma Lazarus wrote "The New Colossus" to support the building of a pedestal for the Statue of Liberty. The poem's closing lines are now inscribed on that monument's base.

The New Colossus

Not like the brazen giant of Greek fame,
With conquering limbs astride from land to
 land;
Here at our sea-washed, sunset gates shall stand
A mighty woman with a torch, whose flame
Is the imprisoned lightning, and her name
Mother of Exiles. From her beacon-hand

Glows world-wide welcome; her mild eyes com-
   mand
The air-bridged harbor that twin cities frame.
"Keep, ancient lands, your storied pomp!" cries
   she
With silent lips. "Give me your tired, your poor,
Your huddled masses yearning to breathe free,
The wretched refuse of your teeming shore.
Send these, the homeless, tempest-tost to me,
I lift my lamp beside the golden door!"

Ella Wheeler Wilcox (1850–1919)

A prolific author throughout her life, Ella
Wilcox wrote her first novel at the age of nine.
Her sentimental and passionate verse was pub-
lished in newspapers and magazines throughout
America, garnering a readership almost un-
equalled in her time.

Solitude

Laugh, and the world laughs with you;
   Weep, and you weep alone.
For the sad old earth must borrow its mirth,
   But has trouble enough of its own.
Sing, and the hills will answer;
   Sigh, it is lost on the air.
The echoes bound of a joyful sound,
   But shrink from voicing care.

Rejoice, and men will seek you;
　　Grieve, and they turn and go.
They want full measure of all your pleasure,
　　But they do not need your woe.
Be glad, and your friends are many;
　　Be sad, and you lose them all.
There are none to decline your nectared wine,
　　But alone you must drink life's gall.

Feast, and your halls are crowded;
　　Fast, and the world goes by.
Succeed and give, and it helps you live,
　　But no man can help you die.
There is room in the halls of pleasure
　　For a long and lordly train,
But one by one we must all file on
　　Through the narrow aisles of pain.

The Winds of Fate

One ship drives east and another drives west
　　With the selfsame winds that blow.
　　　　'Tis the set of the sails
　　　　And not the gales
　　Which tells us the way to go.

Like the winds of the sea are the ways of fate,
　　As we voyage along through life:
　　　　'Tis the set of a soul
　　　　That decides its goal,
　　And not the calm or the strife.

Ernest Lawrence Thayer (1863–1940)

First published under a pseudonym in the San Francisco *Examiner* in 1888, Thayer's "Casey at the Bat" has become an American standard and an unofficial anthem of baseball.

Casey at the Bat

The outlook wasn't brilliant for the Mudville
   nine that day;
The score stood four to two with but one inning
   more to play.
And then when Cooney died at first, and
   Barrows did the same,
A sickly silence fell upon the patrons of the game.

A straggling few got up to go in deep despair.
   The rest
Clung to the hope which springs eternal in the
   human breast;
They thought if only Casey could but get a
   whack at that—
We'd put up even money now with Casey at the
   bat.

But Flynn preceded Casey, as did also Jimmy
   Blake,
And the former was a lulu and the latter was a
   cake;
So upon that stricken multitude grim melan-
   choly sat,

For there seemed but little chance of Casey's getting to the bat.

But Flynn let drive a single, to the wonderment of all,
And Blake, the much despis-ed, tore the cover off the ball;
And when the dust had lifted, and the men saw what had occurred,
There was Johnnie safe at second and Flynn a-hugging third.

Then from 5,000 throats and more there rose a lusty yell;
It rumbled through the valley, it rattled in the dell;
It knocked upon the mountain and recoiled upon the flat,
For Casey, mighty Casey, was advancing to the bat.

There was ease in Casey's manner as he stepped into his place;
There was pride in Casey's bearing and a smile on Casey's face.
And when, responding to the cheers, he lightly doffed his hat,
No stranger in the crowd could doubt 'twas Casey at the bat.

Ten thousand eyes were on him as he rubbed his hands with dirt;

Five thousand tongues applauded when he
 wiped them on his shirt.
Then while the writhing pitcher ground the ball
 into his hip,
Defiance gleamed in Casey's eye, a sneer curled
 Casey's lip.

And now the leather-covered sphere came
 hurtling through the air,
And Casey stood a-watching it in haughty
 grandeur there.
Close by the sturdy batsman the ball unheeded
 sped—
"That ain't my style," said Casey. "Strike one,"
 the umpire said.

From the benches, black with people, there went
 up a muffled roar,
Like the beating of the storm-waves on a stern
 and distant shore.
"Kill him! Kill the umpire!" shouted some one
 on the stand;
And it's likely they'd have killed him had not
 Casey raised his hand.

With a smile of Christian charity great Casey's
 visage shown;
He stilled the rising tumult; he bade the game go
 on;
He signaled to the pitcher, and once more the
 spheroid flew;

But Casey still ignored it, and the umpire said,
  "Strike two."

"Fraud!" cried the maddened thousands, and
  echo answered fraud;
But one scornful look from Casey and the audi-
  ence was awed.
They saw his face grow stern and cold, they saw
  his muscles strain,
And they knew that Casey wouldn't let that ball
  go by again.

The sneer is gone from Casey's lip, his teeth are
  clenched in hate;
He pounds with cruel violence his bat upon the
  plate.
And now the pitcher holds the ball, and now he
  lets it go,
And now the air is shattered by the force of
  Casey's blow.

Oh, somewhere in this favored land the sun is
  shining bright;
The band is playing somewhere, and somewhere
  hearts are light,
And somewhere men are laughing, and some-
  where children shout;
But there is no joy in Mudville—mighty Casey
  has struck out.

Edgar Lee Masters (1868–1950)

Masters' *Spoon River Anthology* (from which the following is taken) recreates the intrigues, feuds, triumphs, and defeats of life in a small Midwestern town, told in the self-written epitaphs of its dead.

The Unknown

Ye aspiring ones, listen to the story of the unknown
Who lies here with no stone to mark the place.
As a boy reckless and wanton,
Wandering with gun in hand through the forest
Near the mansion of Aaron Hatfield,
I shot a hawk perched on the top
Of a dead tree.
He fell with guttural cry
At my feet, his wing broken.
Then I put him in a cage
Where he lived many days cawing angrily at me
When I offered him food.
Daily I search the realms of Hades
For the soul of the hawk,
That I may offer him the friendship
Of one whom life wounded and caged.

Edwin Arlington Robinson (1869–1935)

Robinson's best-known poems, like those of Edgar Lee Masters, reflect life in a small American town. His elevated diction and precise metrical technique, however, stand in marked contrast to the rough voice and liberated form used by Masters.

Miniver Cheevy

Miniver Cheevy, child of scorn,
    Grew lean while he assailed the seasons;
He wept that he was ever born,
    And he had reasons.

Miniver loved the days of old
    When swords were bright and steeds were
      prancing;
The vision of a warrior bold
    Would set him dancing.

Miniver sighed for what was not,
    And dreamed, and rested from his labors;
He dreamed of Thebes and Camelot,
    And Priam's neighbors.

Miniver mourned the ripe renown
    That made so many a name so fragrant;
He mourned Romance, now on the town,
    And Art, a vagrant.

Miniver loved the Medici,
  Albeit he had never seen one;
He would have sinned incessantly
  Could he have been one.

Miniver cursed the commonplace
  And eyed a khaki suit with loathing;
He missed the mediæval grace
  Of iron clothing.

Miniver scorned the gold he sought,
  But sore annoyed was he without it;
Miniver thought, and thought, and thought,
  And thought about it.

Miniver Cheevy, born too late,
  Scratched his head and kept on thinking;
Miniver coughed, and called it fate,
  And kept on drinking.

Mr. Flood's Party

Old Eben Flood, climbing alone one night
Over the hill between the town below
And the forsaken upland hermitage
That held as much as he should ever know
On earth again of home, paused warily.
The road was his with not a native near;
And Eben, having leisure, said aloud,
For no man else in Tilbury Town to hear:

"Well, Mr. Flood, we have the harvest moon
Again, and we may not have many more;

The bird is on the wing, the poet says,
And you and I have said it here before.
Drink to the bird." He raised up to the light
The jug that he had gone so far to fill,
And answered huskily: "Well, Mr. Flood,
Since you propose it, I believe I will."

Alone, as if enduring to the end
A valiant armor of scarred hopes outworn,
He stood there in the middle of the road
Like Roland's ghost winding a silent horn.
Below him, in the town among the trees,
Where friends of other days had honored him,
A phantom salutation of the dead
Rang thinly till old Eben's eyes were dim.

Then, as a mother lays her sleeping child
Down tenderly, fearing it may awake,
He set the jug down slowly at his feet
With trembling care, knowing that most things
     break;
And only when assured that on firm earth
It stood, as the uncertain lives of men
Assuredly did not, he paced away,
And with his hand extended paused again:

"Well, Mr. Flood, we have not met like this
In a long time; and many a change has come
To both of us, I fear, since last it was
We had a drop together. Welcome home!"
Convivially returning with himself,
Again he raised the jug up to the light;

And with an acquiescent quaver said:
"Well, Mr. Flood, if you insist, I might.

"Only a very little, Mr. Flood—
For auld lang syne. No more, sir; that will do."
So, for the time, apparently it did,
And Eben evidently thought so too;
For soon amid the silver loneliness
Of night he lifted up his voice and sang,
Secure, with only two moons listening,
Until the whole harmonious landscape rang—

"For auld lang syne." The weary throat gave out,
The last word wavered, and the song was done.
He raised again the jug regretfully
And shook his head, and was again alone.
There was not much that was ahead of him,
And there was nothing in the town below—
Where strangers would have shut the doors
That many friends had opened long ago.

Richard Cory

Whenever Richard Cory went down town,
We people on the pavement looked at him:
He was a gentleman from sole to crown,
Clean favored, and imperially slim.

And he was always quietly arrayed,
And he was always human when he talked;
But still he fluttered pulses when he said,
"Good-morning," and he glittered when he
   walked.

And he was rich—yes, richer than a king—
And admirably schooled in every grace;
In fine, we thought that he was everything
To make us wish that we were in his place.

So on we worked, and waited for the light,
And went without the meat, and cursed the bread;
And Richard Cory, one calm summer night,
Went home and put a bullet through his head.

Reuben Bright

Because he was a butcher and thereby
Did earn an honest living (and did right),
I would not have you think that Reuben Bright
Was any more a brute than you or I;
For when they told him that his wife must die,
He stared at them, and shook with grief and fright,
And cried like a great baby half that night,
And made the women cry to see him cry.

And after she was dead, and he had paid
The singers and the sexton and the rest,
He packed a lot of things that she had made
Most mournfully away in an old chest
Of hers, and put some chopped-up cedar boughs
In with them, and tore down the slaughter-house.

Stephen Crane (1871–1900)

Despite the success of his early novel *The Red Badge of Courage,* Stephen Crane was largely neglected as a poet during his lifetime. The twentieth century, however, has come to recognize in Crane's verse the work of a writer near to Whitman and Dickinson in the originality of his form and vision.

'I saw a man pursuing the horizon'

I saw a man pursuing the horizon;
Round and round they sped.

I was disturbed at this;
I accosted the man.
"It is futile," I said,
"You can never——"

"You lie," he cried,
And ran on.

War Is Kind

Do not weep, maiden, for war is kind.
Because your lover threw wild hands toward the
    sky
And the affrighted steed ran on alone,
Do not weep.
War is kind.

Hoarse, booming drums of the regiment,
Little souls who thirst for fight,
These men were born to drill and die.
The unexplained glory flies above them,

Great is the battle-god, great, and his king-
    dom——
A field where a thousand corpses lie.

Do not weep, babe, for war is kind.
Because your father tumbled in the yellow
    trenches,
Raged at his breast, gulped and died,
Do not weep.
War is kind.

Swift blazing flag of the regiment,
Eagle with crest of red and gold,
These men were born to drill and die.
Point for them the virtue of slaughter,
Make plain to them the excellence of killing
And a field where a thousand corpses lie.

Mother whose heart hung humble as a button
On the bright splendid shroud of your son,
Do not weep.
War is kind.

James Weldon Johnson (1871–1938)

An educator, diplomat, and NAACP general
secretary, Johnson wrote poetry that ranged
from sonnets in standard English to verse in the
dialect of the South. He also edited the seminal
anthology *The Book of American Negro Poetry*
(1921; rev. 1931).

Sence You Went Away

Seems lak to me de stars don't shine so bright,
Seems lak to me de sun done loss his light,
Seems lak to me der's nothin' goin' right,
    Sence you went away.

Seems lak to me de sky ain't half so blue,
Seems lak to me dat ev'ything wants you,
Seems lak to me I don't know what to do,
    Sence you went away.

Seems lak to me dat ev'ything is wrong,
Seems lak to me de day's jes twice es long,
Seems lak to me de bird's forgot his song,
    Sence you went away.

Seems lak to me I jes can't he'p but sigh,
Seems lak to me ma th'oat keeps gittin' dry,
Seems lak to me a tear stays in ma eye,
    Sence you went away.

Paul Laurence Dunbar (1872–1906)

Dunbar's dialect poems brought him a readership unprecedented for a black poet. Today, however, his reputation rests primarily upon his poetry in traditional English, in which he addresses issues of identity and prejudice.

The Lesson

My cot was down by a cypress grove,
  And I sat by my window the whole night long,
And heard well up from the deep dark wood
  A mocking-bird's passionate song.

And I thought of myself so sad and lone,
  And my life's cold winter that knew no spring;
Of my mind so weary and sick and wild,
  Of my heart too sad to sing.

But e'en as I listened the mocking-bird's song,
  A thought stole into my saddened heart,
And I said, "I can cheer up some other soul
  By a carol's simple art."

For oft from the darkness of hearts and lives
  Come songs that brim with joy and light,
As out of the gloom and the cypress grove
  The mocking-bird sings at night.

So I sang a lay for a brother's ear
  In a strain to soothe his bleeding heart,
And he smiled at the sound of my voice and lyre,
  Though mine was a feeble art.

But at his smile I smiled in turn,
  And into my soul there came a ray:
In trying to soothe another's woes
  Mine own had passed away.

Sympathy

I know what the caged bird feels, alas!
　When the sun is bright on the upland slopes;
When the wind stirs soft through the springing
　　grass
And the river flows like a stream of glass;
　When the first bird sings and the first bud opes,
And the faint perfume from its chalice steals—
I know what the caged bird feels!

I know why the caged bird beats his wing
　Till blood is red on the cruel bars;
For he must fly back to his perch and cling
When he fain would be on the bough a-swing;
　And a pain still throbs in the old, old scars
And they pulse again with a keener sting—
I know why he beats his wing!

I know why the caged bird sings, ah me,
　When his wing is bruised and his bosom sore,—
When he beats his bars and would be free;
It is not a carol of joy or glee,
　But a prayer that he sends from his heart's
　　deep core,
But a plea, that upward to Heaven he flings—
I know why the caged bird sings!

We Wear the Mask

We wear the mask that grins and lies,
It hides our cheeks and shades our eyes—

This debt we pay to human guile;
With torn and bleeding hearts we smile
And mouth with myriad subtleties.

Why should the world be over-wise,
In counting all our tears and sighs?
Nay, let them only see us, while
   We wear the mask.

We smile, but oh great Christ, our cries
To Thee from tortured souls arise.
We sing, but oh the clay is vile
Beneath our feet, and long the mile;
But let the world dream otherwise,
   We wear the mask!

Gertrude Stein (1874–1946)

Working in almost every verbal medium, Gertrude Stein strove to free words from their traditional (and in her mind, stale) associations. Her poetic portraits, like the Cubist paintings she admired, are intended to capture the "essence" of her subjects without the use of conventional methods of representation.

Susie Asado

Sweet sweet sweet sweet sweet tea.
   Susie Asado.
Sweet sweet sweet sweet sweet tea.
   Susie Asado.

Susie Asado which is a told tray sure.

A lean on the shoe this means slips slips hers.

When the ancient light grey is clean it is yellow, it is a silver seller.

This is a please this is a please there are the saids to jelly. These are the wets these say the sets to leave a crown to Incy.

Incy is short for incubus.

A pot. A pot is a beginning of a rare bit of trees. Trees tremble, the old vats are in bobbles, bobbles which shade and shove and render clean, render clean must.

Drink pups.

Drink pups drink pups lease a sash hold, see it shine and a bobolink has pins. It shows a nail.

What is a nail. A nail is unison.

Sweet sweet sweet sweet sweet tea.

Robert Frost (1874–1963)

Though often considered the quintessential poet of New England and America, Frost was raised in California and first published in England. His poems, written mostly in plain speech using a traditional meter, frequently compare the outer, natural world to the inner world of the psyche.

After Apple-Picking

My long two-pointed ladder's sticking through
  a tree
Toward heaven still,
And there's a barrel that I didn't fill
Beside it, and there may be two or three
Apples I didn't pick upon some bough.
But I am done with apple-picking now.
Essence of winter sleep is on the night,
The scent of apples: I am drowsing off.
I cannot rub the strangeness from my sight
I got from looking through a pane of glass
I skimmed this morning from the drinking trough
And held against the world of hoary grass.
It melted, and I let it fall and break.
But I was well
Upon my way to sleep before it fell,
And I could tell
What form my dreaming was about to take.
Magnified apples appear and disappear,
Stem end and blossom end,
And every fleck of russet showing clear.
My instep arch not only keeps the ache,
It keeps the pressure of the ladder-round.
I feel the ladder sway as the boughs bend.
And I keep hearing from the cellar bin
The rumbling sound
Of load on load of apples coming in.
For I have had too much

Of apple-picking: I am overtired
Of the great harvest I myself desired.
There were ten thousand thousand fruit to touch,
Cherish in hand, lift down, and not let fall.
For all
That struck the earth,
No matter if not bruised or spiked with stubble,
Went surely to the cider-apple heap
As of no worth.
One can see what will trouble
This sleep of mine, whatever sleep it is.
Were he not gone,
That woodchuck could say whether it's like his
Long sleep, as I describe its coming on,
Or just some human sleep.

Birches

When I see birches bend to left and right
Across the lines of straighter darker trees,
I like to think some boy's been swinging them.
But swinging doesn't bend them down to stay
As ice-storms do. Often you must have seen them
Loaded with ice a sunny winter morning
After a rain. They click upon themselves
As the breeze rises, and turn many-colored
As the stir cracks and crazes their enamel.
Soon the sun's warmth makes them shed crystal
    shells
Shattering and avalanching on the snow-crust—
Such heaps of broken glass to sweep away

You'd think the inner dome of heaven had fallen.
They are dragged to the withered bracken by the
   load,
And they seem not to break; though once they
   are bowed
So low for long, they never right themselves:
You may see their trunks arching in the woods
Years afterwards, trailing their leaves on the ground
Like girls on hands and knees that throw their hair
Before them over their heads to dry in the sun.
But I was going to say when Truth broke in
With all her matter-of-fact about the ice-storm
I should prefer to have some boy bend them
As he went out and in to fetch the cows—
Some boy too far from town to learn baseball,
Whose only play was what he found himself,
Summer or winter, and could play alone.
One by one he subdued his father's trees
By riding them down over and over again
Until he took the stiffness out of them,
And not one but hung limp, not one was left
For him to conquer. He learned all there was
To learn about not launching out too soon
And so not carrying the tree away
Clear to the ground. He always kept his poise
To the top branches, climbing carefully
With the same pains you use to fill a cup
Up to the brim, and even above the brim.
Then he flung outward, feet first, with a swish,

Kicking his way down through the air to the
   ground.
So was I once myself a swinger of birches.
And so I dream of going back to be.
It's when I'm weary of considerations,
And life is too much like a pathless wood
Where your face burns and tickles with the cob-
   webs
Broken across it, and one eye is weeping
From a twig's having lashed across it open.
I'd like to get away from earth awhile
And then come back to it and begin over.
May no fate willfully misunderstand me
And half grant what I wish and snatch me away
Not to return. Earth's the right place for love:
I don't know where it's likely to go better.
I'd like to go by climbing a birch tree,
And climb black branches up a snow-white trunk
Toward heaven, till the tree could bear no more,
But dipped its top and set me down again.
That would be good both going and coming back.
One could do worse than be a swinger of birches.

Mending Wall

Something there is that doesn't love a wall,
That sends the frozen-ground-swell under it,
And spills the upper boulders in the sun;
And makes gaps even two can pass abreast.
The work of hunters is another thing:

I have come after them and made repair
Where they have left not one stone on a stone,
But they would have the rabbit out of hiding,
To please the yelping dogs. The gaps I mean,
No one has seen them made or heard them made,
But at spring mending-time we find them there.
I let my neighbor know beyond the hill;
And on a day we meet to walk the line
And set the wall between us once again.
We keep the wall between us as we go.
To each the boulders that have fallen to each.
And some are loaves and some so nearly balls
We have to use a spell to make them balance:
"Stay where you are until our backs are turned!"
We wear our fingers rough with handling them.
Oh, just another kind of out-door game,
One on a side. It comes to little more:
There where it is we do not need the wall:
He is all pine and I am apple orchard.
My apple trees will never get across
And eat the cones under his pines, I tell him.
He only says, "Good fences make good neigh-
    bors."
Spring is the mischief in me, and I wonder
If I could put a notion in his head:
"*Why* do they make good neighbors? Isn't it
Where there are cows? But here there are no cows.
Before I built a wall I'd ask to know
What I was walling in or walling out,
And to whom I was like to give offense.

Something there is that doesn't love a wall,
That wants it down." I could say "Elves" to him,
But it's not elves exactly, and I'd rather
He said it for himself. I see him there
Bringing a stone grasped firmly by the top
In each hand, like an old-stone savage armed.
He moves in darkness as it seems to me,
Not of woods only and the shade of trees.
He will not go behind his father's saying,
And he likes having thought of it so well
He says again, "Good fences make good neigh-
  bors."

The Road Not Taken

Two roads diverged in a yellow wood,
And sorry I could not travel both
And be one traveler, long I stood
And looked down one as far as I could
To where it bent in the undergrowth;

Then took the other, as just as fair,
And having perhaps the better claim,
Because it was grassy and wanted wear;
Though as for that the passing there
Had worn them really about the same,

And both that morning equally lay
In leaves no step had trodden black.
Oh, I kept the first for another day!
Yet knowing how way leads on to way,
I doubted if I should ever come back.

I shall be telling this with a sigh
Somewhere ages and ages hence:
Two roads diverged in a wood, and I—
I took the one less traveled by,
And that has made all the difference.

A Patch of Old Snow

There's a patch of old snow in a corner
    That I should have guessed
Was a blow-away paper the rain
    Had brought to rest.

It is speckled with grime as if
    Small print overspread it,
The news of a day I've forgotten—
    If I ever read it.

Carl Sandburg (1878–1967)

Although clearly influenced by Whitman's free verse and celebration of the common man, Sandburg's own use of language and subject matter also derived from his experiences as a manual laborer in the Midwest. Sandburg ultimately received three Pulitzer prizes: one for his multi-volume biography of Abraham Lincoln, and two for his poetry.

Chicago

Hog Butcher for the World,
Tool Maker, Stacker of Wheat,
Player with Railroads and the Nation's
    Freight Handler;
Stormy, husky, brawling,
City of the Big Shoulders:

They tell me you are wicked and I believe them,
    for I have seen your painted women under the
    gas lamps luring the farm boys.
And they tell me you are crooked and I answer:
    Yes, it is true I have seen the gunman kill and
    go free to kill again.
And they tell me you are brutal and my reply is:
    On the faces of women and children I have
    seen the marks of wanton hunger.
And having answered so I turn once more to
    those who sneer at this my city, and I give
    them back the sneer and say to them:
Come and show me another city with lifted head
    singing so proud to be alive and coarse and
    strong and cunning.
Flinging magnetic curses amid the toil of piling
    job on job, here is a tall bold slugger set vivid
    against the little soft cities;
Fierce as a dog with tongue lapping for action,
    cunning as a savage pitted against the wilder-
    ness,

Bareheaded,
Shoveling,
Wrecking,
Planning,
Building, breaking, rebuilding,
Under the smoke, dust all over his mouth,
    laughing with white teeth,
Under the terrible burden of destiny laughing as
    a young man laughs,
Laughing even as an ignorant fighter laughs
    who has never lost a battle,
Bragging and laughing that under his wrist is
    the pulse, and under his ribs the heart of the
    people,
            Laughing!
Laughing the stormy, husky, brawling laughter
    of Youth, half-naked, sweating, proud to be
Hog Butcher, Tool Maker, Stacker of Wheat,
Player with Railroads and Freight Handler to
    the Nation.

Fog

The fog comes
on little cat feet.

It sits looking
over harbor and city
on silent haunches
and then moves on.

I Am the People, the Mob

I am the people—the mob—the crowd—the mass.

Do you know that all the great work of the world is done through me?

I am the workingman, the inventor, the maker of the world's food and clothes.

I am the audience that witnesses history. The Napoleons come from me and the Lincolns. They die. And then I send forth more Napoleons and Lincolns.

I am the seed ground. I am a prairie that will stand for much plowing. Terrible storms pass over me. I forget. The best of me is sucked out and wasted. I forget. Everything but Death comes to me and makes me work and give up what I have. And I forget.

Sometimes I growl, shake myself and spatter a few red drops for history to remember. Then—I forget.

When I, the People, learn to remember, when I, the People, use the lessons of yesterday and no longer forget who robbed me last year, who played me for a fool—then there will be no speaker in all the world say the name: "The People," with any fleck of a sneer in his voice or any far-off smile of derision.

The mob—the crowd—the mass—will arrive then.

The Harbor

Passing through huddled and ugly walls
By doorways where women
Looked from their hunger-deep eyes,
Haunted with shadows of hunger-hands,
Out from the huddled and ugly walls,
I came sudden, at the city's edge,
On a blue burst of lake,
Long lake waves breaking under the sun
On a spray-flung curve of shore;
And a fluttering storm of gulls,
Masses of great gray wings
And flying white bellies
Veering and wheeling free in the open.

Vachel Lindsay (1879–1931)

Lindsay began his poetic career by tramping
around the country, bartering his verse for food
and shelter. He believed that poetry was best ex-
perienced when read aloud, and he frequently
chose themes that had a strong popular appeal.

Abraham Lincoln Walks at Midnight
(In Springfield, Illinois)

It is portentous, and a thing of state
That here at midnight, in our little town
A mourning figure walks, and will not rest,
Near the old court-house pacing up and down,

Or by his homestead, or in shadowed yards
He lingers where his children used to play,
Or through the market, on the well-worn stones
He stalks until the dawn-stars burn away.

A bronzed, lank man! His suit of ancient black,
A famous high top-hat and plain worn shawl
Make him the quaint great figure that men love,
The prairie-lawyer, master of us all.

He cannot sleep upon his hillside now,
He is among us:—as in times before!
And we who toss and lie awake for long,
Breathe deep, and start, to see him pass the door.

His head is bowed. He thinks on men and kings.
Yea, when the sick world cries, how can he sleep?
Too many peasants fight, they know not why;
Too many homesteads in black terror weep.

The sins of all the war-lords burn his heart.
He sees the dreadnaughts scouring every main.
He carries on his shawl-wrapped shoulders now
The bitterness, the folly and the pain.

He cannot rest until a spirit-dawn
Shall come;—the shining hope of Europe free:
The league of sober folk, the Workers' Earth,
Bringing long peace to Cornland, Alp and Sea.

It breaks his heart that kings must murder still,
That all his hours of travail here for men

Seem yet in vain. And who will bring white peace
That he may sleep upon his hill again?

Euclid

Old Euclid drew a circle
On a sand-beach long ago.
He bounded and enclosed it
With angels thus and so.
His set of solemn greybeards
Nodded and argued much
Of arc and of circumference,
Diameter and such.
A silent child stood by them
From morning until noon
Because they drew such charming
Round pictures of the moon.

The Leaden-Eyed

Let not young souls be smothered out before
They do quaint deeds and fully flaunt their pride.
It is the world's one crime its babes grow dull,
Its poor are oxlike, limp and leaden-eyed.
Not that they starve, but starve so dreamlessly;
Not that they sow, but that they seldom reap;
Not that they serve, but have no gods to serve;
Not that they die, but that they die like sheep.

Wallace Stevens (1879–1955)

Stevens was a seeming contradiction: an insurance executive who was also one of this century's most challenging poets. Central to his work is a faith in the redemptive power of the imagination, as well as the conviction that ultimately "Poetry is the subject of the poem."

The Emperor of Ice-Cream

Call the roller of big cigars,
The muscular one, and bid him whip
In kitchen cups concupiscent curds.
Let the wenches dawdle in such dress
As they are used to wear, and let the boys
Bring flowers in last month's newspapers.
Let be be finale of seem.
The only emperor is the emperor of ice-cream.

Take from the dresser of deal,
Lacking the three glass knobs, that sheet
On which she embroidered fantails once
And spread it so as to cover her face.
If her horny feet protrude, they come
To show how cold she is, and dumb.
Let the lamp affix its beam.
The only emperor is the emperor of ice-cream.

Gubbinal

That strange flower, the sun,
Is just what you say.
Have it your way.

The world is ugly,
And the people are sad.

That tuft of jungle feathers,
That animal eye,
Is just what you say.

That savage of fire,
That seed,
Have it your way.

The world is ugly,
And the people are sad.

Thirteen Ways of Looking at a Blackbird

I

Among twenty snowy mountains,
The only moving thing
Was the eye of the blackbird.

II

I was of three minds,
Like a tree
In which there are three blackbirds.

III

The blackbird whirled in the autumn winds.
It was a small part of the pantomime.

IV

A man and a woman
Are one.
A man and a woman and a blackbird
Are one.

V

I do not know which to prefer,
The beauty of inflections
Or the beauty of innuendoes,
The blackbird whistling
Or just after.

VI

Icicles filled the long window
With barbaric glass.
The shadow of the blackbird
Crossed it, to and fro.
The mood
Traced in the shadow
An indecipherable cause.

VII

O thin men of Haddam,
Why do you imagine golden birds?
Do you not see how the blackbird

Walks around the feet
Of the women about you?

VIII

I know noble accents
And lucid, inescapable rhythms;
But I know, too,
That the blackbird is involved
In what I know.

IX

When the blackbird flew out of sight,
It marked the edge
Of one of many circles.

X

At the sight of the blackbirds
Flying in a green light,
Even the bawds of euphony
Would cry out sharply.

XI

He rode over Connecticut
In a glass coach.
Once, a fear pierced him,
In that he mistook
The shadow of his equipage
For blackbirds.

XII

The river is moving.
The blackbird must be flying.

XIII

It was evening all afternoon.
It was snowing
And it was going to snow.
The blackbird sat
In the cedar-limbs.

Disillusionment of Ten O'Clock

The houses are haunted
By white night-gowns.
None are green,
Or purple with green rings,
Or green with yellow rings,
Or yellow with blue rings,
None of them are strange,
With socks of lace
And beaded ceintures.
People are not going
To dream of baboons and periwinkles.
Only, here and there, an old sailor,
Drunk and asleep in his boots,
Catches tigers
In red weather.

William Carlos Williams (1883–1963)

"No ideas but in things," wrote Williams, suggesting his concern with imagery and the immanence of meaning in the ordinary. In following his own dictum, he created a distinctly American art, achieving this in part by his use of the vocabulary and cadences of everyday speech.

The Great Figure

Among the rain
and lights
I saw the figure 5
in gold
on a red
firetruck
moving
tense
unheeded
to gong clangs
siren howls
and wheels rumbling
through the dark city.

The Widow's Lament in Springtime

Sorrow is my own yard
where the new grass
flames as it has flamed
often before but not

with the cold fire
that closes round me this year.
Thirtyfive years
I lived with my husband.
The plumtree is white today
with masses of flowers.
Masses of flowers
load the cherry branches
and color some bushes
yellow and some red
but the grief in my heart
is stronger than they
for though they were my joy
formerly, today I notice them
and turn away forgetting.
Today my son told me
that in the meadows,
at the edge of the heavy woods
in the distance, he saw
trees of white flowers.
I feel that I would like
to go there
and fall into those flowers
and sink into the marsh near them.

Danse Russe

If I when my wife is sleeping
and the baby and Kathleen
are sleeping
and the sun is a flame-white disc

in silken mists
above shining trees,—
if I in my north room
dance naked, grotesquely
before my mirror
waving my shirt round my head
and singing softly to myself:
"I am lonely, lonely.
I was born to be lonely.
I am best so!"
If I admire my arms, my face
my shoulders, flanks, buttocks
against the yellow drawn shades,—

who shall say I am not
the happy genius of my household?

Tract

I will teach you my townspeople
how to perform a funeral—
for you have it over a troop
of artists—
unless one should scour the world—
you have the ground sense necessary.
See! the hearse leads.
I begin with a design for a hearse.
For Christ's sake not black—
nor white either—and not polished!
Let it be weathered—like a farm wagon—
with gilt wheels (this could be

applied fresh at small expense)
or no wheels at all:
a rough day to drag over the ground.

Knock the glass out!
My God—glass, my townspeople!
For what purpose? Is it for the dead
to look out or for us to see
how well he is housed or to see
the flowers or the lack of them—
or what?
To keep the rain and snow from him?
He will have a heavier rain soon:
pebbles and dirt and what not.
Let there be no glass—
and no upholstery phew!
and no little brass rollers
and small easy wheels on the bottom—
my townspeople what are you thinking of?

A rough plain hearse then
with gilt wheels and no top at all
On this the coffin lies
by its own weight.

                No wreathes please—
especially no hot house flowers.
Some common memento is better,
something he prized and is known by:
his old clothes—a few books perhaps—
God knows what! You realize

how we are about these things
my townspeople—
something will be found—anything
even flowers if he had come to that.
So much for the hearse.
For heaven's sake though see to the driver!
Take off the silk hat! In fact
that's no place at all for him—
up there unceremoniously
dragging our friend out to his own dignity!
Bring him down—bring him down!
Low and inconspicuous! I'd not have him ride
on the wagon at all—damn him—
the undertaker's understrapper!
Let him hold the reins
and walk at the side
and inconspicuously too!

Then briefly as to yourselves:
Walk behind—as they do in France,
seventh class, or if you ride
Hell take curtains! Go with some show
of inconvenience; sit openly—
to the weather as to grief.
Or do you think you can shut grief in?
What—from us? We who have perhaps
nothing to lose? Share with us
share with us—it will be money
in your pockets.
      Go now
I think you are ready.

Ezra Pound (1885–1972)

One of the most controversial figures of his time, Ezra Pound exerted a profound influence on American letters, both through his own writing and through his encouragement of other authors (particularly Robert Frost and T. S. Eliot).

The River-Merchant's Wife: A Letter
Translated from the Chinese of Li Po [Rihaku]

While my hair was still cut straight across my
    forehead
I played about the front gate, pulling flowers.
You came by on bamboo stilts, playing horse,
You walked about my seat, playing with blue
    plums.
And we went on living in the village of Chokan:
Two small people, without dislike or suspicion.

At fourteen I married My Lord you.
I never laughed, being bashful.
Lowering my head, I looked at the wall.
Called to, a thousand times, I never looked back.

At fifteen I stopped scowling,
I desired my dust to be mingled with yours
Forever and forever and forever.
Why should I climb the look out?

At sixteen you departed,
You went into far Ku-to-yen, by the river of
    swirling eddies,

And you have been gone five months.
The monkeys make sorrowful noise overhead.
You dragged your feet when you went out.
By the gate now, the moss is grown, the different
    mosses,
Too deep to clear them away!
The leaves fall early this autumn, in wind.
The paired butterflies are already yellow with
    August
Over the grass in the West garden;
They hurt me. I grow older.
If you are coming down through the narrows of
    the river Kiang,
Please let me know beforehand,
And I will come out to meet you
        As far as Cho-fu-Sa.

T. S. Eliot (1888–1965)

Eliot's poems—and especially his fragmented, complex, and highly allusive *The Waste Land*—helped define the modernist movement and twentieth-century poetry as a whole. The only American-born poet to win the Nobel Prize for Literature (1948), Eliot had assumed British citizenship by the time the prize was awarded.

The Love Song of J. Alfred Prufrock

S'io credesse che mia risposta fosse
A persona che mai tornasse al mondo,

Questa fiamma staria senza piu scosse.
Ma perciocche giammai di questo fondo
Non torno vivo alcun, s'i'odo il vero,
Senza tema d'infamia ti rispondo.

Dante Alighieri, *Inferno*

Let us go then, you and I,
When the evening is spread out against the sky
Like a patient etherised upon a table;
Let us go, through certain half-deserted streets,
The muttering retreats
Of restless nights in one-night cheap hotels
And sawdust restaurants with oyster-shells:
Streets that follow like a tedious argument
Of insidious intent
To lead you to an overwhelming question . . .
Oh, do not ask, "What is it?"
Let us go and make our visit.

In the room the women come and go
Talking of Michelangelo.

The yellow fog that rubs its back upon the win-
    dow-panes,
The yellow smoke that rubs its muzzle on the
    window-panes,
Licked its tongue into the corners of the
    evening,
Lingered upon the pools that stand in drains,
Let fall upon its back the soot that falls from
    chimneys,

Slipped by the terrace, made a sudden leap,
And seeing that it was a soft October night,
Curled once about the house, and fell asleep.

And indeed there will be time
For the yellow smoke that slides along the street,
Rubbing its back upon the window-panes;
There will be time, there will be time
To prepare a face to meet the faces that you meet;
There will be time to murder and create,
And time for all the works and days of hands
That lift and drop a question on your plate;
Time for you and time for me,
And time yet for a hundred indecisions,
And for a hundred visions and revisions,
Before the taking of a toast and tea.

In the room the women come and go
Talking of Michelangelo.

And indeed there will be time
To wonder, "Do I dare?" and, "Do I dare?"
Time to turn back and descend the stair,
With a bald spot in the middle of my hair—
(They will say: "How his hair is growing thin!")
My morning coat, my collar mounting firmly to
　the chin,
My necktie rich and modest, but asserted by a
　simple pin—
(They will say: "But how his arms and legs are
　thin!")

Do I dare
Disturb the universe?
In a minute there is time
For decisions and revisions which a minute will
    reverse.

For I have known them all already, known them
    all—
Have known the evenings, mornings, afternoons,
I have measured out my life with coffee spoons;
I know the voices dying with a dying fall
Beneath the music from a farther room.
    So how should I presume?

And I have known the eyes already, known them
    all—
The eyes that fix you in a formulated phrase,
And when I am formulated, sprawling on a pin,
When I am pinned and wriggling on the wall,
Then how should I begin
To spit out all the butt-ends of my days and ways?
    And how should I presume?

And I have known the arms already, known
    them all—
Arms that are braceleted and white and bare
(But in the lamplight, downed with light brown
    hair!)
Is it perfume from a dress
That makes me so digress?
Arms that lie along a table, or wrap about a shawl.

And should I then presume?
And how should I begin?

*   *   *

Shall I say, I have gone at dusk through narrow
    streets
And watched the smoke that rises from the pipes
Of lonely men in shirt-sleeves, leaning out of
    windows? . . .

I should have been a pair of ragged claws
Scuttling across the floor of silent seas.

*   *   *

And the afternoon, the evening, sleeps so peace-
    fully!
Smoothed by long fingers,
Asleep . . . tired . . . or it malingers,
Stretched on the floor, here beside you and me.
Should I, after tea and cakes and ices,
Have the strength to force the moment to its cri-
    sis?
But though I have wept and fasted, wept and
    prayed,
Though I have seen my head (grown slightly
    bald) brought in upon a platter,
I am no prophet—and here's no great matter;
I have seen the moment of my greatness flicker,
And I have seen the eternal Footman hold my
    coat, and snicker,
And in short, I was afraid.

And would it have been worth it, after all,
After the cups, the marmalade, the tea,
Among the porcelain, among some talk of you
   and me,
Would it have been worth while,
To have bitten off the matter with a smile,
To have squeezed the universe into a ball
To roll it toward some overwhelming question,
To say: "I am Lazarus, come from the dead,
Come back to tell you all, I shall tell you all"—
If one, settling a pillow by her head,
   Should say: "That is not what I meant at all.
   That is not it, at all."

And would it have been worth it, after all,
Would it have been worth while,
After the sunsets and the dooryards and the
   sprinkled streets,
After the novels, after the teacups, after the
   skirts that trail along the floor—
And this, and so much more?—
It is impossible to say just what I mean!
But as if a magic lantern threw the nerves in pat-
   terns on a screen:
Would it have been worth while
If one, settling a pillow or throwing off a shawl,
And turning toward the window, should say:
   "That is not it at all,
   That is not what I meant, at all."

*   *   *

No! I am not Prince Hamlet, nor was meant to
    be;
Am an attendant lord, one that will do
To swell a progress, start a scene or two,
Advise the prince; no doubt, an easy tool,
Deferential, glad to be of use,
Politic, cautious, and meticulous;
Full of high sentence, but a bit obtuse;
At times, indeed, almost ridiculous—
Almost, at times, the Fool.

I grow old . . . I grow old . . .
I shall wear the bottoms of my trousers rolled.
Shall I part my hair behind? Do I dare to eat a
    peach?
I shall wear white flannel trousers, and walk
    upon the beach.
I have heard the mermaids singing, each to each.

I do not think that they will sing to me.

I have seen them riding seaward on the waves
Combing the white hair of the waves blown back
When the wind blows the water white and black.

We have lingered in the chambers of the sea
By sea-girls wreathed with seaweed red and brown
Till human voices wake us, and we drown.

Gerontion

Thou hast nor youth nor age
But as it were an after dinner sleep
Dreaming of both

Here I am, an old man in a dry month,
Being read to by a boy, waiting for rain.
I was neither at the hot gates
Nor fought in the warm rain
Nor knee deep in the salt marsh, heaving a cutlass,
Bitten by flies, fought.
My house is a decayed house,
And the jew squats on the window sill, the owner,
Spawned in some estaminet of Antwerp,
Blistered in Brussels, patched and peeled in
  London.
The goat coughs at night in the field overhead;
Rocks, moss, stonecrop, iron, merds.
The woman keeps the kitchen, makes tea,
Sneezes at evening, poking the peevish gutter.
                              I an old man,
A dull head among windy spaces.

  Signs are taken for wonders. "We would see a
    sign":
The word within a word, unable to speak a word,
Swaddled with darkness. In the juvescence of
  the year
Came Christ the tiger

In depraved May, dogwood and chestnut,
    flowering judas,
To be eaten, to be divided, to be drunk
Among whispers; by Mr. Silvero
With caressing hands, at Limoges
Who walked all night in the next room;

    By Hakagawa, bowing among the Titians;
By Madame de Tornquist, in the dark room
Shifting the candles; Fraulein von Kulp
Who turned in the hall, one hand on the door.
    Vacant shuttles
Weave the wind. I have no ghosts,
An old man in a draughty house
Under a windy knob.

    After such knowledge, what forgiveness?
    Think now
History has many cunning passages, contrived
    corridors
And issues, deceives with whispering ambitions,
Guides us by vanities. Think now
She gives when our attention is distracted
And what she gives, gives with such supple con-
    fusions
That the giving famishes the craving. Gives too
    late
What's not believed in, or if still believed,
In memory only, reconsidered passion. Gives
    too soon

Into weak hands, what's thought can be dis-
   pensed with
Till the refusal propagates a fear. Think
Neither fear nor courage saves us. Unnatural
   vices
Are fathered by our heroism. Virtues
Are forced upon us by our impudent crimes.
These tears are shaken from the wrath-bearing
   tree.

   The tiger springs in the new year. Us he de-
      vours. Think at last
We have not reached conclusion, when I
Stiffen in a rented house. Think at last
I have not made this show purposelessly
And it is not by any concitation
Of the backward devils.
I would meet you upon this honestly.
I that was near your heart was removed there-
   from
To lose beauty in terror, terror in inquisition.
I have lost my passion: why should I need to
   keep it
Since what is kept must be adulterated?
I have lost my sight, smell, hearing, taste and
   touch:
How should I use them for your closer contact?

   These with a thousand small deliberations
Protract the profit of their chilled delirium,

Excite the membrane, when the sense has cooled,
With pungent sauces, multiply variety
In a wilderness of mirrors. What will the spider
  do,
Suspend its operations, will the weevil
Delay? De Bailhache, Fresca, Mrs. Cammel,
  whirled
Beyond the circuit of the shuddering Bear
In fractured atoms. Gull against the wind, in the
  windy straits
Of Belle Isle, or running on the Horn,
White feathers in the snow, the Gulf claims,
And an old man driven by the Trades
To a sleepy corner.

                Tenants of the house,
Thoughts of a dry brain in a dry season.

Rhapsody on a Windy Night

Twelve o'clock.
Along the reaches of the street
Held in a lunar synthesis,
Whispering lunar incantations
Dissolve the floors of memory
And all its clear relations,
Its divisions and precisions,
Every street-lamp that I pass
Beats like a fatalistic drum,
And through the spaces of the dark
Midnight shakes the memory
As a madman shakes a dead geranium.

Half-past one,
The street-lamp sputtered,
The street-lamp muttered,
The street-lamp said, "Regard that woman
Who hesitates toward you in the light of the door
Which opens on her like a grin.
You see the border of her dress
Is torn and stained with sand,
And you see the corner of her eye
Twists like a crooked pin."

The memory throws up high and dry
A crowd of twisted things;
A twisted branch upon the beach
Eaten smooth, and polished
As if the world gave up
The secret of its skeleton,
Stiff and white.
A broken spring in a factory yard,
Rust that clings to the form that the strength has
    left
Hard and curled and ready to snap.

Half-past two,
The street-lamp said,
"Remark the cat which flattens itself in the gutter,
Slips out its tongue
And devours a morsel of rancid butter."
So the hand of the child, automatic,
Slipped out and pocketed a toy that was running
    along the quay.

I could see nothing behind that child's eye.
I have seen eyes in the street
Trying to peer through lighted shutters,
And a crab one afternoon in a pool,
An old crab with barnacles on his back,
Gripped the end of a stick which I held him.

Half-past three,
The lamp sputtered,
The lamp muttered in the dark.
The lamp hummed:
"Regard the moon,
La lune ne garde aucune rancune,
She winks a feeble eye,
She smiles into corners.
She smooths the hair of the grass.
The moon has lost her memory.
A washed-out smallpox cracks her face,
Her hand twists a paper rose,
That smells of dust and old Cologne,
She is alone
With all the old nocturnal smells
That cross and cross across her brain.
The reminiscence comes
Of sunless dry geraniums
And dust in crevices,
Smells of chestnuts in the streets,
And female smells in shuttered rooms,
And cigarettes in corridors
And cocktail smells in bars."

The lamp said,
"Four o'clock,
Here is the number on the door.
Memory!
You have the key,
The little lamp spreads a ring on the stair.
Mount.
The bed is open; the tooth-brush hangs on the wall,
Put your shoes at the door, sleep, prepare for life."

The last twist of the knife.

Claude McKay (1890–1948)

Born in Jamaica, McKay came to America to
study and remained to write. His poetry collec-
tion *Harlem Shadows* is thought by many critics
to have inaugurated the Harlem Renaissance.

After the Winter

Some day, when trees have shed their leaves
    And against the morning's white
The shivering birds beneath the eaves
    Have sheltered for the night,
We'll turn our faces southward, love,
    Toward the summer isle
Where bamboos spire the shafted grove
    And wide-mouthed orchids smile.

And we will seek the quiet hill
    Where towers the cotton tree,

And leaps the laughing crystal rill,
 And works the droning bee.
And we will build a cottage there
 Beside an open glade,
With black-ribbed bluebells blowing near,
 And ferns that never fade.

If We Must Die

If we must die, let it not be like hogs
Hunted and penned in an unglorious spot,
While round us bark the mad and hungry dogs,
Making their mock at our accursed lot.
If we must die—oh, let us nobly die,
So that our precious blood may not be shed
In vain; then even the monsters we defy
Shall be constrained to honor us though dead!
Oh, Kinsmen! we must meet the common foe;
Though far outnumbered, let us show us brave,
And for their thousand blows deal one death-
 blow!
What though before us lies the open grave?
Like men we'll face the murderous, cowardly pack,
Pressed to the wall, dying, but fighting back!

The Tropics in New York

Bananas ripe and green, and gingerroot,
 Cocoa in pods and alligator pears,
And tangerines and mangoes and grapefruit,
 Fit for the highest prize at parish fairs,

Set in the window, bringing memories
   Of fruit trees laden by low-singing rills,
And dewy dawns, and mystical blue skies
   In benediction over nunlike hills.

My eyes grew dim, and I could no more gaze;
   A wave of longing through my body swept,
And, hungry for the old, familiar ways,
   I turned aside and bowed my head and wept.

Edna St. Vincent Millay (1892–1950)

Millay's poem "Renascence," published when she was twenty, brought her national attention. One of this century's masters of the sonnet form, she was awarded the Pulitzer Prize in 1923.

First Fig

My candle burns at both ends;
   It will not last the night;
But ah, my foes, and oh, my friends—
   It gives a lovely light.

Recuerdo

We were very tired, we were very merry—
We had gone back and forth all night on the ferry.
It was bare and bright, and smelled like a stable—
But we looked into a fire, we leaned across a table,
We lay on a hill-top underneath the moon;

And the whistles kept blowing, and the dawn
   came soon.

We were very tired, we were very merry—
We had gone back and forth all night on the ferry;
And you ate an apple, and I ate a pear,
From a dozen of each we had bought somewhere;
And the sky went wan, and the wind came cold,
And the sun rose dripping, a bucketful of gold.

We were very tired, we were very merry,
We had gone back and forth all night on the ferry.
We hailed, "Good-morrow, mother!" to a shawl-
   covered head,
And bought a morning paper, which neither of
   us read;
And she wept, "God bless you!" for the apples
   and pears,
And we gave her all our money but our subway
   fares.

Spring

To what purpose, April, do you return again?
Beauty is not enough.
You can no longer quiet me with the redness
Of little leaves opening stickily.
I know what I know.
The sun is hot on my neck as I observe
The spikes of the crocus.
The smell of the earth is good.
It is apparent that there is no death.

But what does that signify?
Not only under ground are the brains of men
Eaten by maggots.
Life in itself
Is nothing,
An empty cup, a flight of uncarpeted stairs.
It is not enough that yearly, down this hill,
April
Comes like an idiot, babbling and strewing
    flowers.

Alphabetical List of Authors, Titles, and First Lines